Editor
Eric Migliaccio

Cover Artist
Brenda DiAntonis

Illustrators
Clint McKnight
Mark Mason

Editor in Chief
Ina Massler Levin, M.A.

Creative Director
Karen J. Goldfluss, M.S. Ed.

Art Coordinator
Renée Christine Yates

Imaging
Rosa C. See
James Edward Grace

Publisher

Mary D. Smith, M.S. Ed.

Differentiated Lessons and Assessments

SCIENCE

Includes Standards & Benchmarks

Grade **6**

Focuses on:
- Reading Strategies
- Content Specific Vocabulary
- Multiple Assessment Options
- Activities for Various Learning Styles
- Graphic Organizers

Author

Julia McMea[...]

Teacher Created Resources, Inc.
6421 Industry Way
Westminster, CA 92683
www.teachercreated.com
ISBN: 978-1-4206-2926-2

© *2010 Teacher Created Resources, Inc.*
Made in U.S.A.

Teacher Created Resources

Table of Contents

Table of Contents *(cont.)*

Table of Contents *(cont.)*

Introduction to Differentiated Instruction

 ## What is differentiated instruction?

Just when you thought it was safe to go back into the classroom, yet another new teaching strategy emerges which will demand more of your time, more of your energy, and endless hours of professional development. Just kidding!

The truth is that the only thing new about differentiated instruction is the name "differentiated instruction"—for teachers know that every time they give a student a few extra minutes to take a test or allow a child to draw a response (as opposed to writing one), they have differentiated their instruction. Simply put, differentiated instruction means that the instruction of the core content, the student activities, and the assessments are modified to meet the individual needs, styles, and abilities of students.

 ## How is instruction differentiated?

Instruction may be differentiated or modified using multiple criteria, including (but not limited to) learning style, reading level, interest, ability, and language. In addition, an educator may differentiate all components of the lesson—content delivery, student activities, and assessment—or only some of them.

 ## How can this book help?

This book contains a lot strategies, activities, assessments, and resources, but how you use them will be your decision. Some of them you will be familiar with, others you will not be. Some will work for your students, and others won't. No one knows your students as well as you do, so ultimately you will decide what you can and cannot use.

This book is intended to help you differentiate your lessons. It is not the last word on the subject of differentiated instruction, nor does it contain every possible strategy known to teacher-kind; it is just one more tool to add to your box.

How This Book Is Organized

This book is divided into nine units. Each unit contains the following sections:

 Teacher Materials

The teacher materials provide the following:

- **Key Unit Concepts:** These are the important ideas, events, and people contained within the student briefs that should be emphasized during the teaching of the unit.

- **Discussion Topics:** These are one or two topics related specifically to the unit that you may use to generate discussion before you begin the unit proper.

- **Assessments:** Here you will find a list of the assessments that are provided for the unit. There are many ways in which to differentiate the assessments. Explanations of these strategies will be cross-referenced with page numbers.

In addition to the above features, the following generic strategies are given on pages 8 and 9. These strategies can be used with each unit and will be referenced in the Teacher Materials section of each unit:

- **Vocabulary Activities/Strategies:** Use this list of suggested activities and strategies to further your students' understanding of the vocabulary words presented in each unit.

- **Building Background:** Here you will find some generic activities and strategies to use before you begin to teach the unit. To avoid repetition at the beginning of each unit, these are cross-referenced with page numbers so that you can find explanations of the activities and strategies.

- **Before, During, and After Reading (BDA):** Here you will find some generic activities and strategies to use before, during, and after students read the briefs. To avoid repetition at the beginning of each unit, these are cross-referenced with page numbers so that you can find explanations of the activities and strategies.

 Unit Activities

The unit activities provide the following:

- **Student Activities:** These are specific activities that students may do after they have read the student briefs. There are a wide variety of activities for visual, logical, verbal, musical, and kinesthetic learners.

- **Key Words:** These are specific words that you may use to search the Internet to find more activities and information related specifically to the content.

- **Activity Centers:** Here you will find some ideas for the creation of activity centers that relate specifically to the unit. Not every unit is accompanied by an activity center.

- **Internet Resources:** Here you will find Internet resources that students may use with the units. Remember, however, that some of these resources may no longer be available at the time you wish to use them. Make sure that you check their availability before you incorporate them into your lesson.

How This Book Is Organized (cont.)

 Student Introductions

These one-page introductions to the unit will give students a quick peek at the information they will encounter. Sometimes the introductions may come in the form of songs, poems, or mnemonic devices. At other times, they might be flow charts, word webs, or other graphic organizers.

 Unit Vocabulary

In this section, vocabulary words for the unit are introduced and defined.

 Assessments

The assessments are designed so that the same content is being tested regardless of the format of the test. Each unit in this book provides these six assessments:

- Multiple Choice
- Matching
- Sentence Completion
- Graphic
- True-False
- Short Response

Modifying the Assessments: You may choose to modify any of these assessments by trying one of the following:

- Give students more time to take the tests.
- Allow students to use the briefs to help answer the questions.
- Audio-record the tests or read the questions aloud to students.
- Allow students to answer the questions orally.

Portfolio Assessment: In addition to one of the traditional assessments, you may also use a portfolio assessment. Select five pieces of work that the student has completed for the unit. Or, you may ask students to select five of their best pieces of work from the unit.

Assessment Rubrics

- *Graphic Assessment:* The rubric on page 213 will help you evaluate these assessments. Graphic assessments provide students with a vehicle to demonstrate their understanding of specific material in a visual context. Because these assessments only evaluate understanding of one specific piece of content, it is recommended that you use this assessment in conjunction with one of the other assessments provided.

- *Short-Response Assessment:* A basic rubric for these assessments is provided on page 214. The short-response assessments provide students with a way to demonstrate such higher-order thinking skills as reasoning, analysis, evaluation and synthesis. Each question is designed to take about five minutes to answer, and students should aim to use 4–6 sentences to answer each question.

 Student Briefs

Each unit provides several student briefs. These briefs contain the core content. They are written with readability in mind, meaning that they use various fonts, bulleted lists, and spacing strategies in order to help struggling readers access the content.

It is important to remember that these briefs are intended to provide students with a very basic, bare-bones presentation of the content. It will be up to you to provide the broader context and to fill in the details. These briefs are also designed to be used alongside your science textbook.

Generic Strategies and Activities

 ## Vocabulary Activities/Strategies

Provide students with a copy of the words, then assign a few of the activities below:

- Draw a picture of the words.
- Scramble the words and swap with a classmate.
- Play hangman with the words.
- Create a bingo game with the words.
- Write a synonym and antonym for the words.
- Act out the words.
- Write the words in a sentence.
- Snap, slap, or stomp out the syllables of the words.
- Read the words aloud.
- Teach the words to someone else.

 ## Building Background Activities/Strategies

Provide students with a copy of the "Student Introduction," then use a few of the strategies below:

- Go over the student introduction teaching students songs, poems, mnemonics, etc.
- Complete word webs to introduce unit concepts.
- Formulate discussion questions to activate background knowledge.
- Select a few of the discussion topics provided and allow students time to discuss.
- Have students use different color highlighter pens to mark content on the student introduction.

 ## Before Reading Activities/Strategies

Provide students with a copy of the "Student Brief," then use a few of the strategies below:

- Direct students' attention to the focus box.
- Show students pictures (if applicable) of the areas of study.
- Point out headings and subheadings to students.
- Have students use different color highlighter pens to highlight headings, subheadings, graphics, etc.
- Remind students that the content vocabulary is in boldfaced print.

Generic Strategies and Activities (cont.)

 During Reading Activities/Strategies

As students read each "Student Brief," use a few of the strategies below:

- Provide students with a copy of "Comprehension Cake" (page 10) so that they can record key information as they read.

- Teach students the SQR3 method:

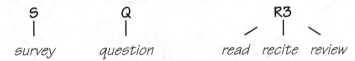

- Use echo reading, choral reading, and/or paired reading.

- Audio-record the briefs and allow students to listen to them.

- Provide quiet corners or headphones for students who have difficulty staying focused.

- Have students use the connection sign when they encounter material that relates to something they already know. (The connection sign is simply interlacing the fingers of each hand.) Ask students to share connections.

 After Reading Activities/Strategies

After students have read the briefs, use a few of the strategies below:

- **Teach Ball:** The teach ball is a large beach ball. Have students stand. Toss the ball to a student and pose a question about the unit. If the student answers correctly, he or she tosses the ball on to another student and asks another unit-related question. If the student doesn't know the answer, he or she says "Pass" and tosses the ball back to you. This can be repeated for several rounds.

- **Speaker's Corner:** Designate a corner of your room as "Speaker's Corner." You can put a little wooden box there on which students can stand. Ask a student to go to the speaker's corner. Ask other students to gather around. Have the student tell what he or she learned from the unit.

- **Review Comprehension Cake:** If "Comprehension Cake" was used, have students share some of the information they recorded.

Usage Tip

At the beginning of each unit, provide each student with a folder. (Preferably, the folder should have pockets, but it can simply be a piece of construction paper folded in half.) Have students write their names on their folders. As students accumulate unit material, have them collect it in their folders.

By the end of the unit, they will have a collection of unit briefs, vocabulary activities, and assessments. The content of this folder can then be used as the basis of a portfolio assessment. As a culminating activity, ask students to decorate their folders in a way that demonstrates what they have learned.

Comprehension Cake

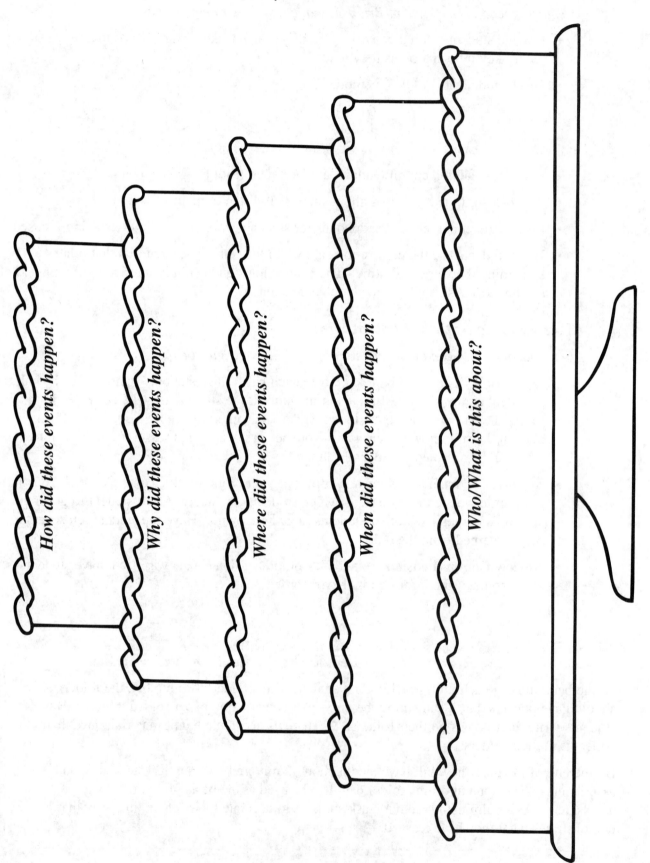

How did these events happen?

Why did these events happen?

Where did these events happen?

When did these events happen?

Who/What is this about?

McREL Content Standards

Listed below are the McREL standards and benchmarks met by the activities in this book.
All standards and benchmarks are used with permission from McREL.
(Copyright 2006 McREL. Mid-continent Research for Education and Learning.
Address: 4601 DTC Boulevard, Suite 500, Denver, CO 80237. Telephone: 303-337-0990.
Website: *www.mcrel.org/standards-benchmarks*

 Earth Science

Standard 2. Understands Earth's composition and structure.

- Knows that the Earth is comprised of layers including a core, mantle, lithosphere, hydrosphere, and atmosphere
- Knows how land forms are created through a combination of constructive and destructive forces
- Knows that the Earth's crust is divided into plates that move at extremely slow rates in response to movements in the mantle
- Knows how successive layers of sedimentary rock and the fossils contained within them can be used to confirm the age, history, and changing life forms on Earth, and how this evidence is affected by the folding, breaking, and uplifting of layers

 Life Sciences

Standard 4. Understands the principles of heredity and related concepts

- Knows that reproduction is a characteristic of all living things and is essential to the continuation of a species
- Knows that for sexual reproducing organisms, a species comprises all organisms that can mate with one another to produce fertile offspring
- Understands asexual reproduction and sexual reproduction
- Knows that hereditary information is contained in genes (located in the chromosomes of each cell), each of which carries a single unit of information; an inherited trait of an individual can be determined by either one of many genes, and a single gene can influence one trait
- Knows that the characteristics of an organism can be described in terms of a combination if traits; some traits are inherited through the coding of genetic material and others result from environmental factors

Standard 5. Understands the structure and function of cells and organisms

- Know that all organisms are composed of cells, which are the fundamental units of life; most organisms are single cells, but other organisms (including humans) are multi-cellular
- Knows that cells convert energy obtained from food to carry on the many functions needed to sustain life
- Knows the levels of organization in living systems, including cells, tissues, organs, organ systems, whole organisms, ecosystems, and the complementary nature of structure and function at each level
- Knows that multi-cellular organisms have a variety of specialized cells, tissues, organs, and organ systems that perform specialized functions and that the function of these systems affects one another

McREL Content Standards *(cont.)*

 Life Sciences *(cont.)*

Standard 5 *(cont.)*

- Knows how an organism's ability to regulate its internal environment enables the organism to obtain and use resources, grow, reproduce, and maintain stable internal conditions while living in a constantly changing external environment
- Knows that organisms can react to internal and environmental stimuli through behavioral response, which may be determined by heredity or from past experience

 Physical Science

Standard 8. Understands the structure and property of matter

- Knows that matter is made up of tiny particles called atoms, and different arrangements of atoms into groups compose all substances
- Knows that elements often combine to form compounds (e.g., molecules, crystals)
- Knows that substances containing only one kind of atom are elements and do not break down by normal laboratory reactions (e.g., heating, exposure to electric current, reaction with acids); over 100 different elements exists
- Knows that many elements can be grouped according to similar properties
- Knows methods used to separate mixtures into their component parts (boiling, filtering, chromatography, screening)

Standard 10. Understands forces and motion

- Understands general concepts related to gravitational force (e.g., every object exerts gravitational force on every other object; this force depends on the mass of the objects and the distance from one another; gravitational force is hard to detect unless at least one of the objects, such as the Earth, has a lot of mass)
- Knows that an object's motion can be described and represented graphically according to its position, direction, and speed
- Understands effects of balanced and unbalanced forces on an object's motion (e.g., if more than one force acts on an object along a straight line, then the forces will reinforce or cancel one another, depending on their direction and magnitude; unbalanced forces, such as friction, will cause changes in the speed or direction of an object's motion)
- Knows that an object that is not being subjected to a force will continue to move at a constant speed and in a straight line

 Scientific Knowledge

Standard 11. Understands the nature of scientific knowledge

- Understands the nature of scientific explanations (e.g., use of logically consistent argument; emphasis on evidence; use of scientific principles, models, and theories; acceptance or displacement of explanations based on new scientific evidence)
- Knows that all scientific ideas are tentative and subject to change and improvement in principle, but for most core ideas in science, there is much experimental and observational confirmation

Cells

Teacher Materials

 Teacher Preperation

Before you begin this unit, photocopy and distribute the following to students:

- Student Introduction (page 15)
- Unit Vocabulary (page 16)
- Student Briefs (pages 17–22)
- Appropriate Assessments (pages 23–34)

 Key Unit Concepts

- *Cells* are the smallest units of life.
- Cells were discovered by the use of a microscope in the 17th century.
- *Cell theory* explains the function of cells and how they reproduce.
- *Multi-cellular* means having many cells.
- *Organelles* are different cell parts that carry out specific jobs that allow the cell to perform its life functions.
- *Diffusion* and *osmosis* are ways in which water, oxygen, and other materials are moved in and out of cells.
- New cells are produced by the division of already existing cells.
- *Mitosis* is when the cell nucleus divides.
- *DNA* is a chemical molecule inside of cells.
- *Chromosomes* are made from DNA.
- *Chromosomes* contain genetic information that determines how cells grow and develop.
- When a cell divides, each new cell gets a copy of all of the pairs of chromosomes.

 Discussion Topics

- Have students provide some examples of discoveries that were only possible because of some breakthrough in technology.
- Cells form a system unto themselves. Have students brainstorm other biological systems.

See "Generic Strategies and Activities" on pages 8 and 9 for additional strategies useful to presenting this unit.

Cells

Activities

 Brief #1: Cell Theory

- **Make an Illustrated Timeline:** Have students research important events and discoveries regarding cells. Using a large piece of butcher paper, ask them to make an illustrated timeline that depicts these events.
- **Write a Biography:** Ask students to select one person who made an important contribution to our understanding of cells. Ask them to write a short biography about that person and include a portrait.
- **Use a Microscope:** Have students look at a variety of slides under a microscope and describe what they see. If a microscope and slides are not available, have students look at magnified images of various living and nonliving things.

  Key Words: *cells, microscopes, Robert Hooke, Anton van Leeuwenhoek, Robert Brown, Matthias Schleiden, Theodore Schwann, Rudolf Virchow, Albrecht van Kolliker, Julius van Sachs, Ernst Ruska, Max Knoll, George E. Palade*

 Brief #2: Organelles

- **Make an Informational Poster:** Using large posterboard and a variety of colored markers, paint, etc., have students make a poster that features an animal cell. Make sure that the relevant cell parts are drawn and labeled.
- **Write a Poem, Song, or Rap:** Have students write a poem, song, or rap that tells the names and job of various animal organelles.
- **Make a Working Model:** Have each student make a working model of the cell membrane and the diffusion process.

  Supplies: small plastic cup, small sandwich bag, cornstarch, iodine, eyedropper, twist tie, water, spoon

  Procedure: Fill the cup halfway with water. Using the eyedropper, add about 10 drops of iodine. Put three spoonfuls of cornstarch into the plastic bag and close the bag with the twist tie. Put the cornstarch bag into the iodine bath. Have students observe the model every five minutes. Eventually, the iodine water will move through the bag and color the cornstarch. Have students use this model and demonstration to explain the process of cell diffusion.

  Key Words: *animal cell, organelles, cell diffusion*

 Brief #3: Cell Division and Reproduction

- **Perform a Skit:** Have students perform a skit that depicts the various phases of mitosis. The skit should include a narrator who talks about each phase as it is being performed.

 Internet Resources

- *http://www.biology4kids.com/* — Biology4Kids website; contains specific information and graphics about cell structure and function
- *http://learn.genetics.utah.edu/content/begin/cells/* — link for "The Science Spot at Kid Zone"; has lots of good information and visuals about cells and other biology topics

Cells

Student Introduction: Cells Word Web

Name: _____ **Date:** _____

Directions: Use this word web to help you brainstorm the characteristics of cells. What do cells do? What are the different parts of a cell?

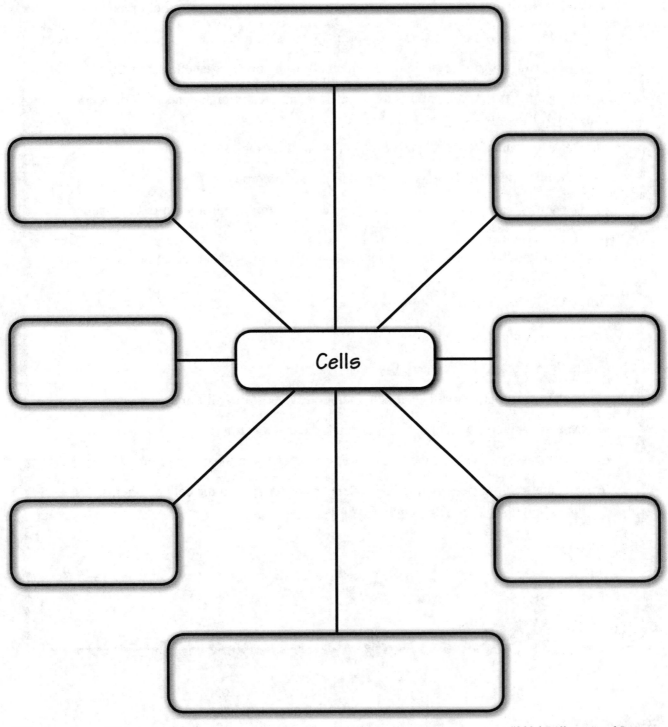

Cells

Vocabulary

1. **cell theory**—a group of observations about the function, behavior, and reproduction of cells

2. **cell membrane**—an organelle that acts as a kind of skin for the other organelles

3. **chromosomes**—tubular structures formed from DNA that are copied during mitosis

4. **cytoplasm**—organelle of liquid in which all of the other organelles are located

5. **diffusion**—the movement of substances from an area of high concentration to an area of low concentration

6. **DNA**—chemical molecule in which cell instructions are stored

7. **endoplasmic reticulum**—organelle that transports proteins

8. **lysosome**—an organelle that has chemicals that help to digest worn-out organelles and other viruses and bacteria that might harm the cell

9. **mitochondria**—organelles that generate chemical energy that the cell uses to power other organelles

10. **mitosis**—division of the cell nucleus

11. **multi-cellular**—having many cells

12. **nucleus**—the control center of the cell

13. **organelles**—parts of cells that help them to carry out their life functions

14. **osmosis**—the movement of water through the cell's membrane

15. **ribosome**—an organelle that begins to turn materials in the cell into protein

16. **vacuole**—an organelle that stores and moves water around the cell, and helps the cell to digest food and eliminate waste materials

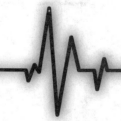

Cells

Brief #1: Cell Theory

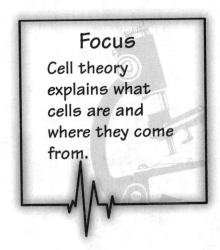

Focus

Cell theory explains what cells are and where they come from.

Cells are the smallest units of life. All living things are made up of cells. But this was not always known to us. Sometimes the discovery of something can only come about because a piece of technology has been invented that allows us to study it. This is what happened with the discovery of cells.

Cells are very small. In fact, they are microscopic. In 1635, a scientist named Robert Hooke made a microscope and looked at a piece of cork through it. Hooke saw that the microscopic piece of cork looked like a honeycomb. It was made of lots of tiny little areas that he called cells.

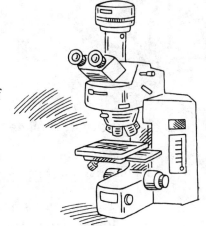

The cells that Hooke observed were not alive. The first person to observe a live cell under a microscope was Anton van Leeuwenhoek. In 1674, he saw a type of algae called spirogyra. He called the tiny moving cells "animalcules."

 Cell Theory

The observations of Hooke, van Leeuwenhoek, and others led to the development of a theory about cells. **Cell theory states the following:**

✓ All living things are made of cells.

✓ Cells are the basic units of living things.

✓ All cells come from existing cells.

Vocabulary

1. cell theory
2. multi-cellular

 What Cells Do

While cells may be microscopic, they perform important and complex functions in living organisms. Cells must get food and nutrients, remove waste from their systems, and grow and reproduce. When cells can't carry out the life functions, they can die.

There are some organisms that are made of one or a few cells. But there are much larger organisms, like humans, who are made up of trillions of cells. **An organism that is made up of many cells is called multi-cellular.** The prefix *multi* means "many."

Cells

Brief #2: Organelles

Cells are made up of different parts that help them to carry out their life functions. A cell's life functions include the following:

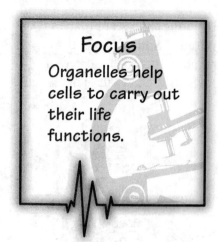

- ✓ eating
- ✓ growing
- ✓ reproducing

The different parts of a cell that help it to carry out these functions are called organelles. You may already know about the organelle called the nucleus. **The nucleus is like the control center of the cell.** But there are many other organelles and each different organelle performs a specific job.

 ### Types of Organelles

Here is a list of other organelles that carry out important functions within the cell. Look at the diagram on page 19 to see how all of these parts fit together.

- ✓ **The endoplasmic reticulum is an organelle that helps to make and transport proteins and sugars around the cell.**

- ✓ **A vacuole is an organelle that stores and moves water around the cell and helps the cell to digest food and eliminate waste materials.**

- ✓ **The ribosome is an organelle that begins to turn materials in the cell into proteins.**

- ✓ **The lysosome is an organelle that has chemicals that help to digest worn-out organelles and other viruses and bacteria that might harm the cell.**

- ✓ **The organelle known as cytoplasm is a kind of liquid in which all of the other organelles are located.**

- ✓ **The cell membrane is an organelle that acts as a kind of skin for the other organelles. It is a barrier that keeps harmful things out of the cell, but it also lets helpful things into the cell.**

- ✓ **The mitochondria is an organelle that generates chemical energy that the cell uses to power other organelles.**

Vocabulary

1. organelles
2. nucleus
3. endoplasmic reticulum
4. vacuole
5. ribosome
6. lysosome
7. cytoplasm
8. cell membrane
9. mitochondria
10. diffusion
11. osmosis

Cells

Brief #2: Organelles *(cont.)*

 Types of Organelles *(cont.)*

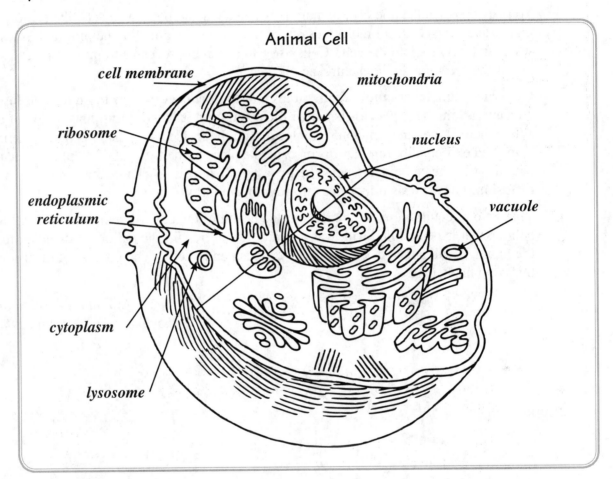

Animal Cell

cell membrane

mitochondria

ribosome

nucleus

endoplasmic
reticulum

vacuole

cytoplasm

lysosome

 Differences Between Cells

Not all cells are exactly the same. The job of the particular cells determines what kinds of organelles it will have. For example, muscle cells have a lot of mitochondrion because they need lots of energy to move. But neurons (nerve cells) have lots of dendrites. Dendrites are like the branches of a tree. They are responsible for sending and receiving chemical signals in the central nervous system.

Plant cells are also different from the cells of animals. A plant cell (pictured to the right) has a cell wall that helps the plant to keep its shape. It also has chloroplasts. These organelles contain the chlorophyll that the plant needs to make its own food.

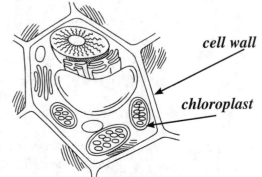

cell wall

chloroplast

Cells

Brief #2: Organelles *(cont.)*

 ### Diffusion and Osmosis

You have learned that the cell membrane is like a barrier, but it also acts like a door. The membrane keeps harmful molecules out of the cell, while allowing helpful molecules, like water and oxygen, into the cell. Cells use two different processes to move molecules in and out of the cell through the membrane.

Generally, substances move from an area of high concentration to an area of low concentration. This process is called diffusion, and it is what happens inside of cells. When there is the same amount of molecules on the inside as on the outside of a cell, the cell is in a state of equilibrium. Diffusion can take place with any kind of helpful molecules that pass through the cell membrane. **The process of osmosis works in the same way as diffusion, but osmosis only refers to the movement of water.**

This state of equilibrium is important to the health of the cell. Imagine that the cell is a balloon that is being filled with water or air. If you overfill the balloon with either the gas or the liquid, it will burst. The same thing can happen in cells. The process of diffusion keeps this from happening.

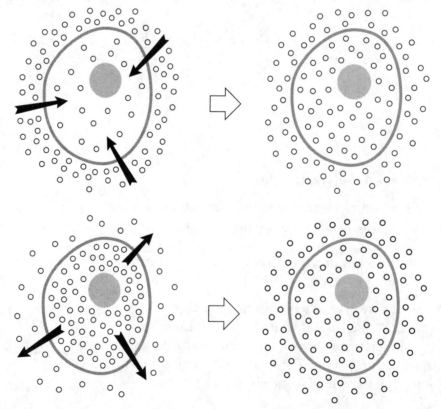

1. *If there are more particles outside the cell...*

2. *they diffuse into the cell until they're evenly distributed.*

3. *If there are more particles inside the cell...*

4. *they move out of the cell until they're evenly distributed.*

Cells

Brief #3: Cell Division and Reproduction

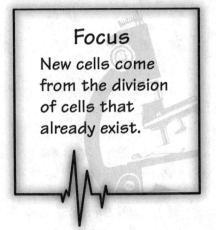

Focus

New cells come from the division of cells that already exist.

It is possible that right at this moment you are over four feet tall. You will continue to grow taller and taller as you age until you stop growing at about the age of 21. But what makes you grow taller and taller with each passing year? The answer is the division of your cells.

Cells are very small—so small that they can't be seen without the aid of a microscope. But your cells have to do all of the same things that your body does to keep you healthy. Cells must take in oxygen and food, and they must remove waste products from their systems.

The tiny size of a cell actually makes it possible for the cell to perform all of these functions. Materials that the cell needs can move from organelle to organelle quickly because the distance between each organelle is so small. If cells continued to get bigger and bigger, it would make these processes more difficult.

Vocabulary

1. DNA

2. mitosis

3. chromosomes

 ### The Division of Cells

If a single cell can only grow so big, then how is that multi-cellular organisms, like us, can grow bigger with age? The answer is that each cell in a multi-cellular organism divides. When a cell divides, it produces an exact duplicate of itself. New cells also replace old cells that are worn out.

Inside the nucleus of every cell is DNA. **DNA is a chemical molecule that stores all of the information and instruction about how the organism will grow and develop.** For instance, the DNA of an elephant is different from the DNA of a shark.

Cell division begins with a process called mitosis. **Mitosis means that the cell nucleus, which contains the DNA, divides. The DNA coils and forms tubular structures called chromosomes.**

Fast Fact

Average Height of an American Male: about 5'9"

Average Height of an American Female: about 5'4"

Chromosomes come in pairs and each living organism has a different number of chromosomes. Human beings have 23 pairs of chromosomes; 46 chromosomes altogether. During mitosis, the nucleus of each new cell receives a full set of chromosomes. Mitosis is complete when the cytoplasm divides. So from one cell, two identical cells are produced. The flow chart on page 22 shows the different steps involved in the production of new cells.

Cells

Brief #3: Cell Division and Reproduction *(cont.)*

 The Division of Cells *(cont.)*

3. *The cytoplasm divided. In animal cells, the cell membrane pinches inward, forming two identical cells. In plant cell, a new cell wall divides one cell into two.*

1. *The cell makes a copy of its DNA and gets ready to divide.*

2a. *Mitosis begins. Chromosomes become visible and the membrane around the nucleus dissolves.*

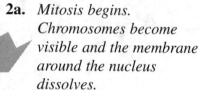

2b. *Pairs of chromosome copies line up at the center of the cell.*

2c. *Each pair of chromosomes separates, and the two halves move to opposite ends of the cell.*

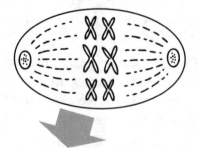

2d. *Mitosis is completed as a new membrane forms around each nucleus.*

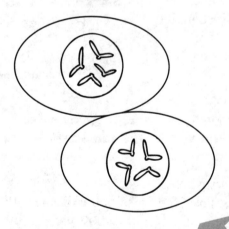

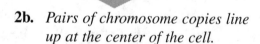

22

Cells

Multiple-Choice Assessment

Name: _____   **Date:** _____

Directions: Read each question carefully. Fill in the correct answer circle.

1. Why didn't people know about cells until the 17th century?
   - Ⓐ They couldn't see them.
   - Ⓑ Cells didn't exist then.
   - Ⓒ Eye glasses had not been invented.
   - Ⓓ none of these

2. What instrument must you use in order to see a cell?
   - Ⓐ telescope
   - Ⓑ thermometer
   - Ⓒ barometer
   - Ⓓ microscope

3. What did Robert Hooke observe that led him to his theories about cells?
   - Ⓐ a human fingernail
   - Ⓑ a human eyelash
   - Ⓒ a piece of cork
   - Ⓓ a spirogyra

4. What did van Leeuwenhoek call "animalcules"?
   - Ⓐ cork
   - Ⓑ spirogyra
   - Ⓒ flat worms
   - Ⓓ dead cells

5. Which of the following is not a part of cell theory?
   - Ⓐ All living things are made of cells.
   - Ⓑ Cells are the basic units of life.
   - Ⓒ Cells are created by osmosis.
   - Ⓓ All cells come from existing cells.

Cells

Multiple-Choice Assessment *(cont.)*

6. *Multi-cellular* means

  Ⓐ "having many cells."

  Ⓑ "being single-celled."

  Ⓒ "plant cells."

  Ⓓ "animal cells."

---

7. What are organelles?

  Ⓐ the cell nucleus

  Ⓑ different parts of a cell

  Ⓒ where the DNA is located

  Ⓓ where the chromosomes are located

---

8. Which of the following is not an organelle?

  Ⓐ DNA molecules

  Ⓑ ribosome

  Ⓒ cell membrane

  Ⓓ vacuole

---

9. What is one of the functions of the cell membrane?

  Ⓐ It produces food.

  Ⓑ It converts light into energy.

  Ⓒ It produces waste products.

  Ⓓ It keeps harmful materials out of the cell.

---

10. Which organelle is responsible for making chemical energy?

  Ⓐ the mitochondria

  Ⓑ the endoplasmic reticulum

  Ⓒ the ribosome

  Ⓓ the cytoplasm

Cells

Multiple-Choice Assessment *(cont.)*

11. What does a plant cell have that an animal cell does not have?

Ⓐ organelles

Ⓑ cytoplasm

Ⓒ nucleus

Ⓓ chloroplasts

---

12. Diffusion is the movement of substances

Ⓐ from an area of low concentration to an area of high concentration.

Ⓑ from a cool area to a warm area.

Ⓒ from an area of high concentration to an area of low concentration.

Ⓓ none of these

---

13. *Osmosis* refers to

Ⓐ the movement of carbon through a cell.

Ⓑ the movement of water through a cell.

Ⓒ the movement of oxygen through a cell.

Ⓓ the division of the cell nucleus.

---

14. How are new cells produced?

Ⓐ by osmosis

Ⓑ by cell division

Ⓒ by diffusion

Ⓓ by recombining DNA

---

15. What is DNA?

Ⓐ a type of cell

Ⓑ a type of nucleus

Ⓒ a type of chromosome

Ⓓ a type of chemical molecule

Cells

Multiple-Choice Assessment *(cont.)*

16. The division of the cell nucleus is called

   Ⓐ osmosis.

   Ⓑ mitosis.

   Ⓒ diffusion.

   Ⓓ collision.

---

17. DNA is formed into

   Ⓐ molecules.

   Ⓑ cells.

   Ⓒ chromosomes.

   Ⓓ none of these.

---

18. When a cell divides, each new cell receives

   Ⓐ one chromosome each.

   Ⓑ improved chromosomes.

   Ⓒ a shared nucleus.

   Ⓓ a full set of chromosomes.

---

19. What signals the completion of mitosis?

   Ⓐ the cytoplasm divides

   Ⓑ the chromosomes are formed

   Ⓒ old cells die

   Ⓓ DNA is expanded

---

20. How many pairs of chromosomes do people have?

   Ⓐ 10

   Ⓑ 15

   Ⓒ 46

   Ⓓ 23

Cells

Sentence-Completion Assessment

Name: _____   **Date:** _____

Directions: Read each statement. Fill in the word or words that best complete the sentence.

1. People first saw cells in the _____ century.

2. In order to see a cell you need to use a _____ .

3. Robert Hooke observed a piece of _____ under a microscope.

4. Anton van Leeuwenhoek called the spirogyra he observed _____ .

5. Scientists developed a _____ about the function of cells and how they reproduce.

6. _____ means an organism that has many cells.

7. An _____ is a part of the cell with a specific job to perform.

8. A _____ stores and moves water around the cell.

9. The _____ is kind of like the skin of the cell.

10. The _____ is responsible for making chemical energy.

11. Chloroplasts can be found only in _____ cells.

Cells

Sentence-Completion Assessment *(cont.)*

12. The movement of substances from an area of high concentration to an area of low concentration is called _____ .

13. The movement of water through a cell is called _____ .

14. New cells are produced when existing cells _____ .

15. The chemical molecule that contains the cell's instructions is called _____ .

16. The division of the cell nucleus is called _____ .

17. _____ are formed from DNA.

18. Mitosis is complete when the _____ divides.

19. Humans have _____ pairs of chromosomes.

20. The _____ is an organelle that digests worn-out organelles.

Cells

True-False Assessment

Name: _____ **Date:** _____

Directions: Read each statement carefully. If the statement is true, put a **T** on the line provided. If the statement is false, put an **F** on the line provided.

_____ **1.** Cells can only be seen though a microscope.

_____ **2.** Robert Hooke observed the dead cells of cork in the 17th century.

_____ **3.** *Animalcules* is Latin for animal.

_____ **4.** Cells are the basic units of life.

_____ **5.** "Multi-cellular" means having two cells.

_____ **6.** Organelles are plant cells.

_____ **7.** A ribosome is a type of organelle.

_____ **8.** Animal cells have cell walls.

_____ **9.** The mitochondria is responsible for producing chemical energy in a cell.

_____ **10.** Plant cells have chloroplasts.

Cells

True-False Assessment *(cont.)*

_____ **11.** Diffusion is the movement of water through cells.

_____ **12.** Osmosis is when the nucleus of a cell divides.

_____ **13.** New cells are produced by the division of existing cells.

_____ **14.** DNA is a chemical molecule.

_____ **15.** Osmosis is the movement of water through the cell membrane.

_____ **16.** Chromosomes are formed from DNA.

_____ **17.** New cells receive a full set of chromosomes.

_____ **18.** Mitosis is complete when the cell membrane collapses.

_____ **19.** Humans have 23 pairs of chromosomes.

_____ **20.** The endoplasmic reticulum digests worn out organelles.

Cells

Matching Assessment

Name: _____   **Date:** _____

Directions: Read the items in both lists below and on page 32 carefully. Choose an item from List B that best matches an item from List A. Write the corresponding letter from List B on the line. You will have some left over.

List A	List B
_____ 1. size of cells	**A.** smallest unit of life
_____ 2. Hooke observation	**B.** chromosomes
_____ 3. animalcules	**C.** cell theory
_____ 4. ideas about cells	**D.** spirogyra
_____ 5. many-celled	**E.** DNA
_____ 6. organelles	**F.** endoplasmic reticulum
_____ 7. vacuole	**G.** completion of mitosis
_____ 8. cell membrane	**H.** energy generator
_____ 9. mitochondria	**I.** multi-cellular
_____ 10. plant cell part	**J.** division of nucleus
_____ 11. high to low concentration	**K.** Anton van Leeuwenhoek
_____ 12. osmosis	**L.** cell skin

GO

Cells

Matching Assessment *(cont.)*

List A	List B
_____ **13.** production of new cells	**M.** division
_____ **14.** chemical molecule	**N.** chloroplast
_____ **15.** mitosis	**O.** water movement
_____ **16.** tubular DNA	**P.** diffusion
_____ **17.** cytoplasm division cells	**Q.** digests worn cells
_____ **18.** 23 in humans	**R.** pairs of chromosomes
_____ **19.** lysosome job	**S.** cork cells
_____ **20.** cell	**T.** water storage
	U. microscopic
	V. cell parts

Cells

Graphic Assessment

Name: _____ **Date:** _____

Directions: Look carefully at the flow chart below. Describe what is happening in each illustration.

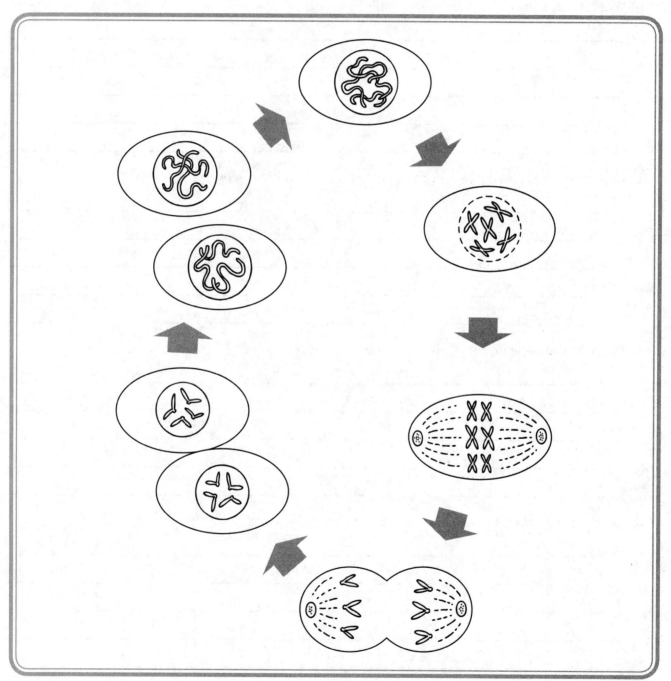

Cells

Short-Response Assessment

Name: _____   **Date:** _____

Directions: Read each question carefully. Write a short response of a few sentences to each question.

1. What is cell theory? Explain how it evolved over time.

   _____

   _____

   _____

   _____

   _____

2. Explain the relationship between technology and scientific discovery.

   _____

   _____

   _____

   _____

   _____

3. Describe diffusion and osmosis.

   _____

   _____

   _____

   _____

4. Describe the process of mitosis.

   _____

   _____

   _____

   _____

The Reproduction of Living Things

Teacher Materials

 Teacher Preparation

Before you begin this unit, photocopy and distribute the following to students:

- Student Introduction (page 38)
- Unit Vocabulary (page 39)
- Student Briefs (pages 40–48)
- Appropriate Assessments (pages 49–61)

 Key Unit Concepts

- Asexual and sexual reproductions are how offspring are produced.
- *Asexual reproduction* requires one parent.
- *Fission, budding, spore formation,* and *fragmentation* are types of asexual reproduction.
- *Sexual reproduction* requires two parents.
- Female sex cells are called *eggs*.
- Male sex cells are called *sperm*.
- *Fertilization* occurs when the sperm and egg cells join together.
- *Meiosis* is the division of a sex cell.
- Sex cells have half of the chromosomes of other cells.
- A sexually produced offspring gets half of its chromosomes from each parent.
- A *zygote* is the first cell produced from fertilization.
- *Genes* are the part of DNA that determine traits.
- Genes are made from the bases A, T, C, and G.
- Genes form rungs in a *double helix* in base pairs.
- During *mitosis*, the bases disconnect and then reconnect.
- A *mutation* is a change in the DNA.
- Genes can be *dominant* or *recessive*.
- Sometimes genes can share dominance.

 Discussion Topics

- Have students discuss what traits they have in common with family members and what traits are unique to them in their families.

> See "Generic Strategies and Activities" on pages 8 and 9 for additional strategies useful to presenting this unit.

The Reproduction of Living Things

Activities

 ### Brief #1: Asexual Reproduction

- **Make an Informational Poster:** Using a large piece of poster board and colored crayons or markers, make a poster that illustrates the various forms of asexual reproduction (fission, budding, spore formation, and fragmentation).

- **Demonstrate Mold Reproduction:**

Supplies: a loaf of white bread, baggies with zipper locks, water

Procedure: After handling a slice of bread liberally with your fingers, put it into a baggie. Add two teaspoonfuls of water, and then close the baggie. Put the baggie in a cool, dark place. After 24 hours, observe the bread. You should be able to see mold spores growing on the bread.

- **Demonstrate Fragmentation:**

Supplies: potatoes, potting soil, plant containers

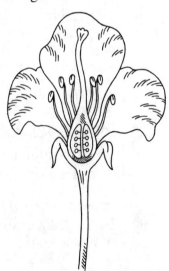

Procedure: Allow the potatoes to sit on a windowsill until they begin to sprout eyes. When the sprouts are about 2 inches in length, break them off of the potato and plant them in a container. Make sure the plants receive enough sunlight and water. After a week, new plants should begin to grow from the fragmented piece.

Key Words: *types of asexual reproduction*

 ### Brief #2: Sexual Reproduction

- **Make a Data Table:** Have students select a total of six organisms that reproduce sexually. Ask them to make a data table that shows the total number of chromosomes in each organism and the number of sex chromosomes in the organism.

- **Make an Informational Poster:** Using a large piece of poster board and colored markers or pencils, make a poster that illustrates a flower and the following parts: pistil, stamen, ovary, embryo, sperm cell, pollen, pollen tube, egg, ovule, and ovary.

Key Words: *parts of a flower, chromosomes in organisms*

The Reproduction of Living Things

Activities *(cont.)*

 Brief #3: Traits and Genes

- **Make a Model of DNA:**

  Supplies: black or red shoestring licorice (two 6-inch-long pieces); red, yellow, blue, and green gumdrops or other jellied candy; toothpicks

  Procedure: Explain that the licorice represents the sides of the DNA ladder and the toothpicks and gumdrops will represent the bases A, T, C, G. Place two strands of the licorice in front of you. Next, take the toothpicks and gumdrops and make some base pairs. Remember that the base pairs in the DNA molecule can only be joined AT, TA, CG, or GC. Attach the base pairs to either end of the licorice strands. Make six rungs on the ladder. Then twist to form the double helix. (See page 45 for an illustration of DNA's double-helix shape.)

- **Invent a Species:** Pretend you are a genetic scientist and you have just landed on the distant planet of Zumto. The Zumtites (the people that live on Zumto) have given you permission to study the genetics of their species. Explain what the Zumtites look like. Tell which Zumtite traits are dominant and which are recessive. Perhaps some Zumtite traits share dominance. Create a poster that illustrates various Zumtites that have these traits. Make sure your poster contains labels.

- **Make a Punnett Square:** Use the following information to construct four Punnett Squares.

  Punnett Square

  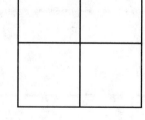

  —*Square 1:* 10 eyes dominant, 2 eyes recessive

  —*Square 2:* plastic hair dominant, aluminum-foil hair recessive

  —*Square 3:* 2 feet dominant, 3 feet recessive

  —*Square 4:* tail dominant, no tail recessive

  Key Words: *Punnett Square, dominant and recessive traits*

 Internet Resources

- *http://www.ornl.gov/sci/techresources/Human_Genome/home.shtml* — official site to the Human Genome Project; includes such teacher and student resources as webcasts, presentations, image galleries, and posters.

- *http://www.pbs.org/wgbh/nova/genome/* — the companion website to Nova's "Cracking the Code of Life"; contains video and information about the Human Genome Project, includes a teacher's guide.

The Reproduction of Living Things

Student Introduction: Reproduction Word Web

Name: _____   **Date:** _____

Directions: Use this word web to help you brainstorm the characteristics of how living things are reproduced.

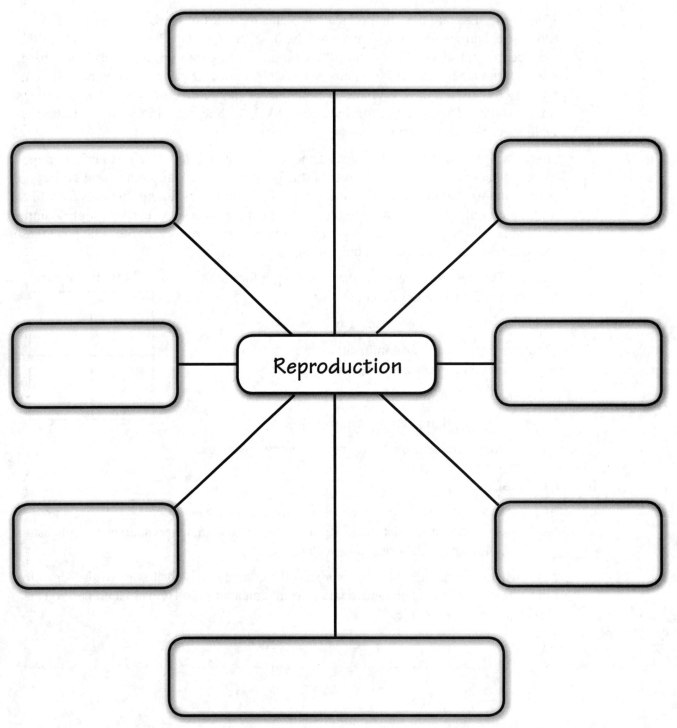

The Reproduction of Living Things

Vocabulary

1. **asexual reproduction**—reproduction of an offspring requiring just one parent

2. **base pairs**—two chemicals bases that join together to form gene in DNA

3. **budding**—type of asexual reproduction in which a parent sprouts a smaller version of itself

4. **double helix**—the shape of a DNA molecule; shaped like a twisted ladder

5. **egg cells**—female sex cells

6. **fertilization**—when an egg and sperm cell join together

7. **fission**—type of asexual reproduction when an organism splits into two identical organisms

8. **fragmentation**—type of asexual reproduction in which an offspring grows from the piece of a parent

9. **gene**—chemical base in DNA that determines traits

10. **meiosis**—the division of a sex cell

11. **mitosis**—process in which the base pairs in a DNA molecule come apart and then form copies of DNA strands with other disconnected bases

12. **sexual reproduction**—reproduction of an offspring requiring two parents

13. **sperm cells**—male sex cells

14. **spore formation**—type of asexual reproduction in which a tiny cell breaks open and releases spores into the atmosphere

15. **zygote**—the first cell that is produced from fertilization

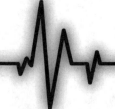

The Reproduction of Living Things

Brief #1: Asexual Reproduction

Focus

During asexual reproduction, only one parent is required.

All living things come from other living things. You came from your parents, and someday you may have children of your own.

There are two different ways in which living things reproduce themselves. One way is called asexual reproduction. **Asexual reproduction means that the offspring of a living organism comes from a single parent and has the exact DNA as the parent.**

Vocabulary

1. asexual reproduction
2. fission
3. budding

 ### Types of Asexual Reproduction

There are several different types of asexual reproduction. In this unit, we will discuss fission, budding, spore formation, and fragmentation.

✓ **Fission**

Microorganisms such as bacteria are reproduced by the process of fission. **During fission, an organism splits into two identical organisms.** Each new organism has the ability to grow to the same size as the original, single parent. The fission process can reproduce organisms very quickly.

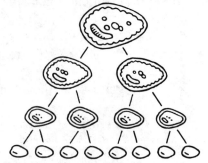

✓ **Budding**

There are many smaller organisms that use the process of budding to reproduce themselves. **During budding, a single parent forms a smaller version of itself that sprouts from its own body.** The bud has the exact same DNA as its parent. Once the bud is large enough, it breaks off of the parent.

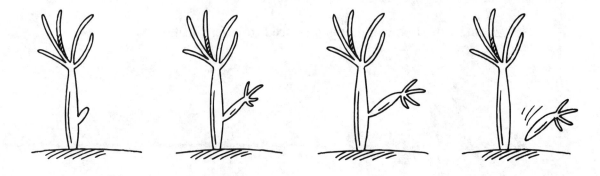

The Reproduction of Living Things

Brief #1: Asexual Reproduction *(cont.)*

 Types of Asexual Reproduction *(cont.)*

✓ **Spore Formation**

There are some types of plants, algae, and fungi that reproduce themselves by a using a process called spore formation.

During spore formation, a tiny cell with a kind of protective coating is produced on the plant, algae, or fungus. When the weather is just right, the spore breaks open and tiny spores are released. These tiny spores have the same DNA as the parent spore. They form new organisms that are identical to the single parent.

spores on a fern plant

✓ **Fragmentation**

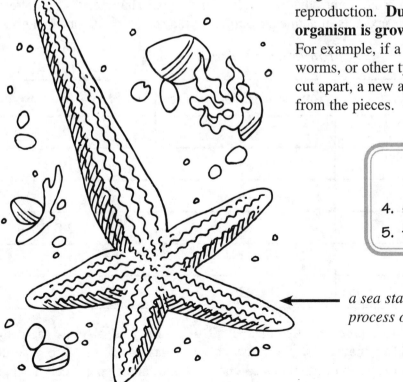

Fragmentation is another type of asexual reproduction. **During fragmentation, a new organism is grown from a part of the parent.** For example, if a sea star, certain kinds of worms, or other types of plants and fungus are cut apart, a new and identical organism can grow from the pieces.

Vocabulary

4. spore formation
5. fragmentation

a sea star undergoing the process of fragmentation

The Reproduction of Living Things

Brief #2: Sexual Reproduction

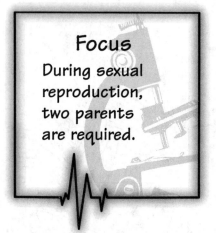

Focus

During sexual reproduction, two parents are required.

Sexual reproduction is a process that requires two parents. **During sexual reproduction, the offspring or new organism gets half of its DNA from one male parent and the other half from one female parent.** The new organism has a combination of DNA, so it is not an exact copy of either one of its parents.

Vocabulary

1. sexual production
2. egg cells
3. sperm cells
4. meiosis
5. fertilization
6. zygote

 Meiosis

Organisms that reproduce sexually have special cells called sex cells. **The sex cells of the female are called egg cells. The sex cells of the male are called sperm cells.**

All of the cells in an organism have a certain number of chromosomes. For example, every cell in the body of a chicken has 78 chromosomes, and every cell in a pineapple has 50 chromosomes.

But sex cells are different from other kinds of cells in an organism. The sex cells only have half of the number of chromosomes that are in the other cells. That means that there are 39 chromosomes in the sex cells of a chicken and 25 in the sex cell of a pineapple.

Chromosomes and Sex Cells

Animal/Plant	Total # of Chromosomes	# of Sex Chromosomes
cabbage	18	9
cat	38	19
dog	78	39
elephant	56	28
human	46	23
yeast	32	16

Sex cells are produced by a process called meiosis. **During meiosis, a single sex cell divides and produces four new cells.** Each new cell only has half of the chromosomes of the parent. So in humans, an egg cell has 23 chromosomes and a sperm cell has 23 chromosomes.

The Reproduction of Living Things

Brief #2: Sexual Reproduction *(cont.)*

 Meiosis *(cont.)*

Sexual reproduction in an organism is when the egg cell and the sperm cell join together. This process is called fertilization. The first new cell that is produced from fertilization is called a zygote. Because the zygote is a combination of two different parents, it has half of the chromosomes from the egg cell and half of the chromosomes from the sperm cell.

Now that the zygote has a full set of chromosomes, it will divide using the process of mitosis and form a new organism.

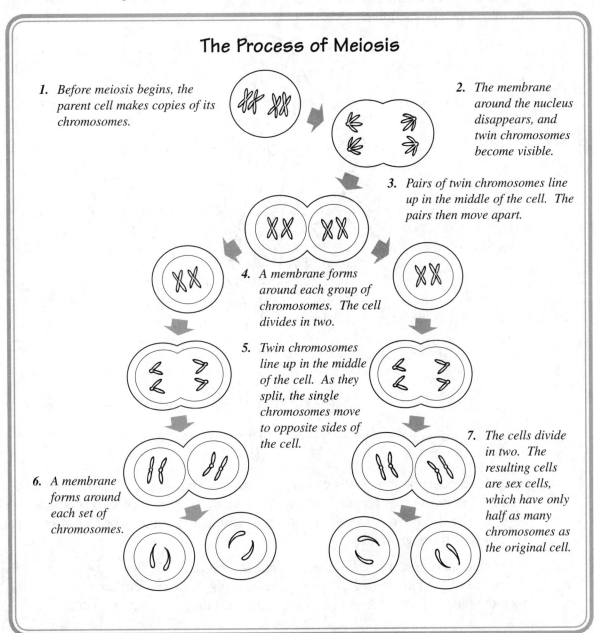

The Process of Meiosis

1. Before meiosis begins, the parent cell makes copies of its chromosomes.

2. The membrane around the nucleus disappears, and twin chromosomes become visible.

3. Pairs of twin chromosomes line up in the middle of the cell. The pairs then move apart.

4. A membrane forms around each group of chromosomes. The cell divides in two.

5. Twin chromosomes line up in the middle of the cell. As they split, the single chromosomes move to opposite sides of the cell.

6. A membrane forms around each set of chromosomes.

7. The cells divide in two. The resulting cells are sex cells, which have only half as many chromosomes as the original cell.

The Reproduction of Living Things

Brief #2: Sexual Reproduction *(cont.)*

 Fertilization

Fertilization can happen in different ways in living things that use sexual reproduction as a method for producing new organisms.

In flowering plants, the sperm cells are located in the pollen. Pollen is the powdery substance that you can often see blowing off of plants. It is produced in the part of the plant called the stamen. A plant's egg cells are produced by the pistil. When pollen is transferred from the stamen to the pistil, pollination (fertilization) has occurred.

The wind and animals like bees, birds, and mammals help to pollinate by carrying pollen from one plant to another.

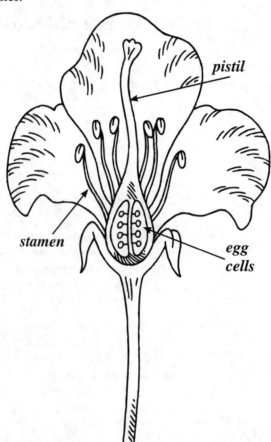

Sexual reproduction in animals can happen inside or outside of the animal's body. For example, in most cases female fish lay eggs outside of their bodies. Then male fish find the eggs and fertilize them. This is true for most animals that live in or close to the water. The water keeps the eggs moist.

Most mammals do not live in water, so fertilization of the egg cells by the sperm happens on the inside of the female body. In reptiles and birds, eggs are fertilized inside of the body, and then the female lays them and cares for them until they are ready to hatch.

The Reproduction of Living Things

Brief #3: Traits and Genes

Focus

Genes and traits are passed from one generation to the next through reproduction.

You have probably noticed that living things look like their parents. Young maple trees look like older maple trees, and you probably look like a combination of your mom and your dad.

But you do not look exactly like them. And if you have brothers and sisters, you know that while you all may resemble one another, each one of you is unique.

Vocabulary

1. double helix

2. gene

3. base pairs

4. mitosis

 DNA

DNA is a chemical molecule that is located in the cells of all living things. Chromosomes are made from DNA. Chromosomes determine what an organism will be. All living things have different numbers of chromosomes. Different numbers of chromosomes produce different type of living things.

The DNA molecule has a definite shape. It is called a double helix. It looks like a kind of twisted ladder. Each rung on this chemical ladder is made up of a gene. **It is the genes that provide the instruction to the cell and determine whether a flower will be red or purple, whether a person will be short or tall, or whether a dog will be black with white patches or white with black patches.**

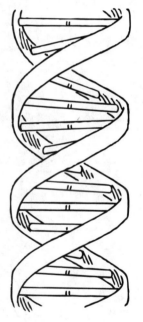

 Base Pairs

DNA is made up of four different chemical bases. These bases are called base A (adenine), base T (thymine), base G (guanine), and base C (cytosine). **The genes in DNA are made up of base pairs.** For example, the base pair TA is a combination of base T and base A.

But these bases that join to form pairs can only join together in certain ways. Bases C and G can only form pairs with each other, and bases A and T can only form pairs together. This is what makes it possible for DNA to copy itself during mitosis. Each rung of the DNA ladder is made up of two base pairs. The ways they are combined determine the traits of a living organism. For example, GC, TA, AT, CG will form a different trait than TA, AT, GC, CG.

The Reproduction of Living Things

Brief #3: Traits and Genes (cont.)

 ## DNA and Mitosis

During mitosis, the base pairs in a DNA molecule come apart. The two strands of DNA are no longer connected by the rungs on the ladder. Each base is now floating around in the cell nucleus. These floating bases find a disconnected strand on the DNA and reconnect. In asexual reproduction, the new strands that are formed are exactly the same as the original DNA. The new organism that is produced will be an exact duplicate of its parent. Sometimes this is called a clone.

Sometimes during sexual reproduction, DNA doesn't copy itself exactly. A change can occur in the way the DNA has been copied. This is called a mutation. Mutations change the instructions in the genes. Mutations can be passed along from one generation to the next.

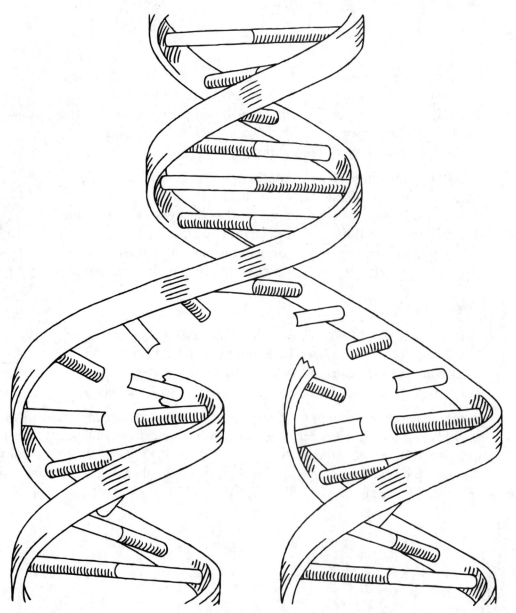

The Reproduction of Living Things

Brief #3: Traits and Genes (cont.)

 ### Traits

You know that during sexual reproduction, an organism receives half of its chromosomes from a female parent and the other half from a male parent. This is why you don't look exactly like your mother or your father but are more of a combination of the two of them.

Each generation of offspring inherits traits from their parents. But what determines which traits are seen and which are not? For example, let's say that a male parent has blue eyes and a female parent has brown eyes. What factors determine what color eyes the offspring will have?

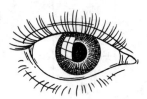 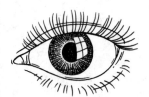

Traits can either be dominant or recessive. If a trait is dominant, it means that it is seen in the offspring. If a trait is recessive, it means that it is not seen. Many traits are made by a pair of genes. If a trait is dominant, it is shown like this: RR. If a trait is recessive, it is shown like this: rr. The chart below shows some common dominant and recessive traits.

So the blue eyes of a male parent is a recessive trait (*rr*), and the brown eyes of a female parent is a dominant trait (*RR*). Any offspring from these two parents will get one copy of the dominant gene (*R*) from their female parent and one copy of the recessive gene (*r*) from their male parent. The offspring will be Rr. In this case, the "R" stands for brown eyes, so the offspring will have brown eyes.

Traits

Dominant (RR)	Recessive (rr)
brown eyes	blue eyes
widow's peak	no widow's peak
six fingers	five fingers
freckles	no freckles

But what might happen if two people, each having one dominant gene for brown eyes and one recessive gene for blue eyes, reproduced? Their offspring would be either *RR, Rr,* or *rr.* Only the *rr* combination would have blue eyes.

If an organism has two copies of the same dominant or recessive gene, it is called purebred. If an organism has one dominant gene and one recessive gene for a trait, then it is called a hybrid.

The Reproduction of Living Things

Brief #3: Traits and Genes *(cont.)*

 Punnett Square

A Punnett square is a diagram that illustrates all of the possible genetic combinations that can occur during sexual reproduction. Let's say that "T" stands for a dominate gene for tallness and that "t" stands for a recessive trait for shortness. The Punnett square below shows the possible outcomes. This pattern is called the dominant-recessive pattern.

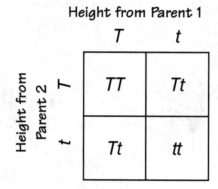

The dominant-recessive pattern is not the only way that genes and their traits can work in an organism. Say, for instance, that both parents of an organism have two recessive traits for a gene. In that case, the genes would have dominance.

Let's say that two black and white cats mated. A black and white cat would have a recessive gene for whiteness and a recessive gene for blackness (wb). What color would the kittens be?

By looking at this Punnett square on the right, you can see the possible outcomes for the color of the kittens.

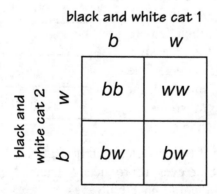

Sometimes when the parents of organisms have two recessive copies of a gene, the traits that are produced are a kind of blend of both. For example, pink flowers are often produced by the sexual reproduction of a white flower and a red flower.

The Reproduction of Living Things

Multiple-Choice Assessment

Name: _____   **Date:** _____

Directions: Read each question carefully. Fill in the correct answer circle.

1. Living organisms reproduce by
   - Ⓐ asexual reproduction.
   - Ⓑ sexual reproduction.
   - Ⓒ unisexual reproduction
   - Ⓓ both A and B

2. The reproduction involving only one parent is called
   - Ⓐ fertilization.
   - Ⓑ mitosis.
   - Ⓒ sexual reproduction.
   - Ⓓ asexual reproduction.

3. Which of the following are types of reproduction?
   - Ⓐ fission
   - Ⓑ fusion
   - Ⓒ fragmentation
   - Ⓓ both A and C

4. What happens during budding?
   - Ⓐ an organism splits into two
   - Ⓑ an organism releases spores
   - Ⓒ a single parent sprouts a smaller version of itself
   - Ⓓ none of these

5. A new organism growing from the pieces of a parent is called
   - Ⓐ fragmentation.
   - Ⓑ budding.
   - Ⓒ fission.
   - Ⓓ spore formation.

The Reproduction of Living Things

Multiple-Choice Assessment *(cont.)*

6. Reproduction which requires one male and one female parent is called

Ⓐ asexual reproduction.

Ⓑ meiosis.

Ⓒ sexual reproduction.

Ⓓ budding.

7. What kinds of sex cells do females have?

Ⓐ sperm cells

Ⓑ egg cells

Ⓒ pollen cells

Ⓓ spore cells

8. How are sex cells different from other cells?

Ⓐ They are larger.

Ⓑ They are smaller.

Ⓒ They have double the chromosomes.

Ⓓ They have half the chromosomes.

9. What is meiosis?

Ⓐ cell division

Ⓑ sex cell division

Ⓒ pollination

Ⓓ chromosome population

10. Sexual reproduction occurs when

Ⓐ an egg and sperm cell join together.

Ⓑ two egg cells join together.

Ⓒ two sperm cells join together.

Ⓓ mitosis is complete.

The Reproduction of Living Things

Multiple-Choice Assessment *(cont.)*

11. What is the first cell produced by sexual reproduction called?

    Ⓐ a coyote

    Ⓑ a zimmo

    Ⓒ an egglet

    Ⓓ a zygote

---

12. Where does a zygote get its chromosomes?

    Ⓐ from the female parent

    Ⓑ from the male parent

    Ⓒ half from the male parent, half from the female parent

    Ⓓ none of these

---

13. Where are the sperm cells located in a flowering plant?

    Ⓐ the bud

    Ⓑ the pollen

    Ⓒ the root

    Ⓓ the pistil

---

14. Where is the pollen produced?

    Ⓐ the stamen

    Ⓑ the pistil

    Ⓒ the leaves

    Ⓓ the vascular root

---

15. Where are the egg cells on a flowering plant located?

    Ⓐ the stamen

    Ⓑ the iris

    Ⓒ the pistil

    Ⓓ all of these

The Reproduction of Living Things

Multiple-Choice Assessment *(cont.)*

16. What is DNA?

    Ⓐ a crystal atom

    Ⓑ a chemical molecule

    Ⓒ a proton

    Ⓓ a cell

17. What shape is DNA?

    Ⓐ a double helix

    Ⓑ a single helix

    Ⓒ a helio-helix

    Ⓓ a ladder

18. What are the rungs on the ladder of DNA made of?

    Ⓐ atoms

    Ⓑ protons

    Ⓒ bacteria

    Ⓓ genes

19. What are the chemical bases of DNA?

    Ⓐ A, B, C, D

    Ⓑ A, T, G, M

    Ⓒ A, R, r, Z

    Ⓓ A, T, G, C

20. How are the genes arranged in the DNA?

    Ⓐ in groups of 3

    Ⓑ in base pairs

    Ⓒ in group of 4

    Ⓓ in a single line

The Reproduction of Living Things

Multiple-Choice Assessment *(cont.)*

21. Which of the following shows an incorrect arrangement of bases?

Ⓐ AG, GC

Ⓑ TA, GC

Ⓒ AT, CG

Ⓓ GC, TA

---

22. What do genes determine?

Ⓐ number of cells

Ⓑ size of cells

Ⓒ amount of blood

Ⓓ traits

---

23. What happens during mitosis?

Ⓐ the base pairs come apart and are then reconnected

Ⓑ the base pairs die

Ⓒ the base pairs undergo a chemical change

Ⓓ all of these

---

24. What is a mutation?

Ⓐ an error in the DNA

Ⓑ an alien form of DNA

Ⓒ a change in the DNA

Ⓓ a type of fish DNA

---

25. What's the difference between a dominant and recessive trait?

Ⓐ a recessive trait can be seen; a dominant trait can't be seen

Ⓑ a recessive gene is a mutation, a dominant gene isn't

Ⓒ a dominant trait can be seen; a recessive trait can't be seen

Ⓓ a dominant trait can kill a recessive trait

The Reproduction of Living Things

Sentence-Completion Assessment

Name: _____   **Date:** _____

Directions: Read each statement. Fill in the word or words that best complete the sentence.

1. Reproduction involving only one parent is called _____ .

2. Reproduction involving two parents is called _____ .

3. During the reproductive process of _____ , an organism splits into two identical organisms.

4. When a single parent sprouts a smaller version of itself it is called _____ .

5. A new organism growing from the piece of a parent is called _____ .

6. Female sex cells are called _____ cells.

7. Male sex cells are called _____ cells.

8. Sex cells have half the _____ of other cells.

9. The division of a sex cell is called _____ .

10. Sexual reproduction occurs when an_____cell

    and a _____ cell join together.

11. The first cell produced by sexual reproduction is called a _____ .

12. The sperm cells of a flowering plant are in the _____ .

The Reproduction of Living Things

Sentence-Completion Assessment *(cont.)*

13. Pollen is produced in the _____ of a flowering plant.

14. The egg cells in a flowering plant are located in the _____ .

15. The chemical molecule that all living things have is called _____ .

16. DNA is shaped like a _____ .

17. The rungs on the ladder of DNA are made of _____ .

18. The chemical bases of DNA are _____, _____,

    _____, and _____ .

19. The genes in DNA are arranged in _____ .

20. The bases AT and _____ go together.

21. Genes determine _____ .

22. During _____ , base pairs are disconnected and then reconnected.

23. A change in the DNA is called a _____ .

24. Genes can be _____ or recessive.

25. An organism with a dominant and recessive gene for the same trait is a _____ .

The Reproduction of Living Things

True-False Assessment

Name: _____ **Date:** _____

Directions: Read each statement carefully. If the statement is true, put a **T** on the line provided. If the statement is false, put an **F** on the line provided.

_____ **1.** Living organisms can reproduce by asexual reproduction.

_____ **2.** Reproduction involving one parent is called sexual reproduction.

_____ **3.** Fragmentation is a type of sexual reproduction.

_____ **4.** During budding a single parent sprouts a smaller version of itself.

_____ **5.** During fission sex cells divide.

_____ **6.** Females have egg cells.

_____ **7.** Sex cells have twice the number of chromosomes as other cells.

_____ **8.** Meiosis is the division of a sex cell.

_____ **9.** Sexual reproduction occurred when two sperm cells join.

_____ **10.** A zygote is the first cell produced by fragmentation.

_____ **11.** A zygote gets half of its chromosomes from a female parent and half from a male parent.

_____ **12.** The sperm cells in a flowering plant are located in the pistil.

56

The Reproduction of Living Things

True-False Assessment *(cont.)*

_____ **13.** Pollen is produced in the buds.

_____ **14.** A flowering plant's egg cells are located in the pistil.

_____ **15.** DNA is a chemical molecule.

_____ **16.** DNA is shaped like a oval.

_____ **17.** The rungs on the ladder of DNA are made of genes.

_____ **18.** The chemical bases of DNA are A, T, C, and G.

_____ **19.** Genes come in base pairs.

_____ **20.** AC and GA are base pairs.

_____ **21.** Traits determine genes.

_____ **22.** During mitosis, base pairs come apart and are reconnected.

_____ **23.** A mutation is an error in the DNA.

_____ **24.** Dominant traits are seen.

_____ **25.** An organism with either two dominant or two recessive genes for the same trait is a purebred.

The Reproduction of Living Things

Matching Assessment

Name: _____   **Date:** _____

Directions: Read the items in both lists below and on page 59 carefully. Choose an item from List B that best matches an item from List A. Write the corresponding letter from List B on the line. You will have some left over.

List A	List B
_____ **1.** sexual reproduction	**A.** spore
_____ **2.** asexual reproduction	**B.** egg producer
_____ **3.** fission reproduction	**C.** seen
_____ **4.** smaller version of parent	**D.** cell division
_____ **5.** new organism from a piece	**E.** sperm
_____ **6.** female sex cells	**F.** DNA
_____ **7.** male sex cells	**G.** fragmentation
_____ **8.** meiosis	**H.** 2 parents
_____ **9.** zygote	**I.** AT, TA
_____ **10.** pollen producer	**J.** recessive trait
_____ **11.** pistil	**K.** 1 parent
_____ **12.** chemical molecule	**L.** first fertilized cell

GO

The Reproduction of Living Things

Matching Assessment *(cont.)*

List A	List B
_____ **13.** shape of DNA	**M.** gene
_____ **14.** trait producer	**N.** Punnett square
_____ **15.** chemical bases	**O.** mutation
_____ **16.** base pairs	**P.** splitting of an organism
_____ **17.** mitosis	**Q.** double helix
_____ **18.** change in DNA	**R.** stamen
_____ **19.** recessive trait	**S.** A, T, C, G
_____ **20.** dominant trait	**T.** pollination
_____ **21.** hybrid	**U.** Rr
_____ **22.** purebred	**V.** budding
_____ **23.** cell with protective coating	**W.** division of sex cell
_____ **24.** blue eyes	**X.** eggs
_____ **25.** plant fertilization	**Y.** RR or rr
	Z. not seen

STOP

The Reproduction of Living Things

Graphic Assessment

Name: _____   **Date:** _____

Directions: Complete the Punnett squares below.

Purple Flowers

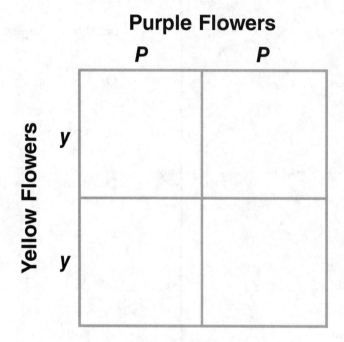

Orange and White Cat

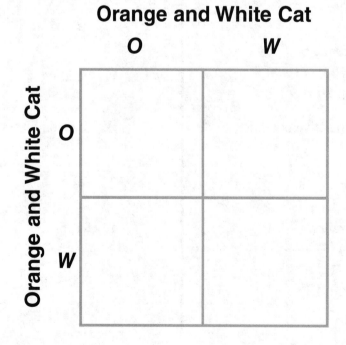

The Reproduction of Living Things

Short-Response Assessment

Name: _____ **Date:** _____

Directions: Read each question carefully. Write a short response of a few sentences to each question.

1. Describe asexual reproduction. Provide examples of this process.

_____

_____

_____

_____

_____

2. Explain the process of meiosis.

_____

_____

_____

_____

_____

3. Describe the DNA molecule. What is it made of? What does it look like?

_____

_____

_____

_____

_____

4. Explain the difference between dominant and recessive traits. What determines which trait shows up in an offspring?

_____

_____

_____

_____

_____

Plants

Teacher Materials

 Teacher Preparation

Before you begin this unit, photocopy and distribute the following to students:

- Student Introduction (page 65)
- Unit Vocabulary (page 66)
- Student Briefs (pages 67–73)
- Appropriate Assessments (pages 74–85)

 Key Unit Concepts

- Roots help to anchor plants in place and draw nutrients and water to other parts of the plant.
- Nutrients and water pass through the *epidermis*.
- The *xylem* moves nutrients from the roots to other parts of the plant.
- The *phloem* distributes sugars to the plant.
- Stems help to support the plant.
- Sugar is produced in the leaves.
- Oxygen and carbon dioxide pass in and out of the *stomata*.
- *Guard cells* open and close the stomata.
- *Transpiration* is when water exits the stomata.
- *Photosynthesis* and *cellular respiration* are opposite processes which make plants and animals interdependent.
- Photosynthesis produces glucose.
- *Angiosperms* are flowering plants.
- *Gymnosperms* are cone-producing trees.
- *Tropism* is a response of a plant to its environment.

 Discussion Topics

- Brainstorm a list of ways in which people use plants to meet their basic needs.
- Speculate about what would happen in a world without plants.

> See "Generic Strategies and Activities" on pages 8 and 9 for additional strategies useful to presenting this unit.

Plants

Activities

 Brief #1: Vascular Plants

- **Observe and Record:** Take a trip to a local nursery or home-and-garden store to have a look at a variety of vascular plants. Have students take notes regarding the types of plants that they see. Are they angiosperms, gymnosperms, perennials, or annuals? Encourage students to look at the plant-care labels to learn about the varying needs of plants.

- **Make an Informational Poster:** Have students create colorful informational posters that illustrate 10 of their favorite foods that are made from vascular plants. Make sure that students include labels on their poster.

- **Research and Report:** Many of the world's most important medicines are made from plants. Have students conduct research into plant-based medicines and write a two-page research report that describes these medications. Students should be encouraged to include illustrations of the plants with their reports.

  Key Words: *plants and medicine*

 Brief #2: Photosynthesis

- **Draw a Diagram:** Have each student draw a diagram that shows the process of cellular respiration. The diagram should depict oxygen and glucose entering a cell, and carbon dioxide, water, and the subsequent energy leaving the cell. Make sure labels are included.

- **Perform an Experiment:** This experiment will demonstrate the location of the stomata on the leaves of plants.

  Supplies: about four or five ordinary houseplants (depending on the size of your class), cotton swabs, petroleum jelly

  Procedure: Using the cotton swabs, coat the topside of a few leaves of the plants with petroleum jelly. Next, coat the underside of different leaves with the same amount of petroleum jelly. Observe the plant each day and record your observations. After one week, draw a conclusion about what you observe.

  Explanation: The leaves with coated undersides will probably be dead. This is because the stomata are located on the underside of the leaves; because they were coated, gases could not move in and out of the leaves.

- **Use a Microscope:** Have students observe the Elodea plant under a microscope using varying magnifications. What parts of the plants can be observed? Ask them to carefully sketch what they see and ask them provide a short written explanation of any movement they observed.

  Key Words: *cellular respiration, Elodea plant*

Plants

Activities *(cont.)*

 Brief #3: Plant Growth

- **Perform an Experiment:** This experiment will demonstrate the importance of light in the growth of plants.

  Supplies: about 20 Styrofoam cups, soil, beans or other fast growing seeds*

  * The seeds need to be all the same, and you will need at least 100 seeds in order to gather enough data for students to draw reasonable conclusions.

  Procedure: Plant seeds in cups. Place the cups in different locations with varying light exposure. You may put some on windowsills that receive direct light, others in places that only receive artificial light, etc. The 20 planted cups should be divided into groups of five. For example, five of the cups may be on a windowsill with direct light. One group containing five cups should be put in a place that doesn't get any light. This is the control group. Have students observe and record their observations. Encourage them to draw conclusions about the impact of light on plant growth.

- **Make a Mural:** Attach a large, long piece of butcher paper to the wall of your classroom. Have students research a variety of angiosperms and gymnosperms and create a colorful mural. Encourage students to include the names of the plants they illustrate.

- **Perform an Experiment:** This experiment will demonstrate two different types of tropism.

  Supplies: pinto beans; small clear, plastic cups; paper towels; masking tape; a marker

  Procedure: Soak the pinto beans overnight. Line the plastic cups with one folded paper towel. Then, crumble up some more paper towels and put them in the plastic cups. These bunched-up towels will hold the folded towels in place. Wet the towels that are in the cups. Pour off as much excess water as possible. Put a piece of masking tape around the top of the cup. Using a marker, make four arrows on the tape. The arrows should point up, down, to the left, and to the right. Put one pinto bean beneath each arrow. The pinto bean should be placed between the plastic cup and the folded paper towel. Before students place their beans, have them locate the hilum, which is the small indentation on the bean. The beans should be placed with the hilum pointing in the direction of the arrow. Moisten the paper towel each day, if needed. Pour off excess water that accumulates at the bottom of the glass. Observe the direction in which the root grows each day. After a week or so, have students explain the direction in which the root grew regardless of the position of the bean.

  Explanation: The roots will grow downward. This is an example of gravitotropism.

 Internet Resources

- *http://www.biology4kids.com/files/plants_main.html* — a kid-friendly site about plants

- *http://www.botany.org/plantimages/* — website for the Botanical Society of America

Plants

Student Introduction: Plants Word Web

Name: _____ **Date:** _____

Directions: Use this word web to help you brainstorm the characteristics of plants.

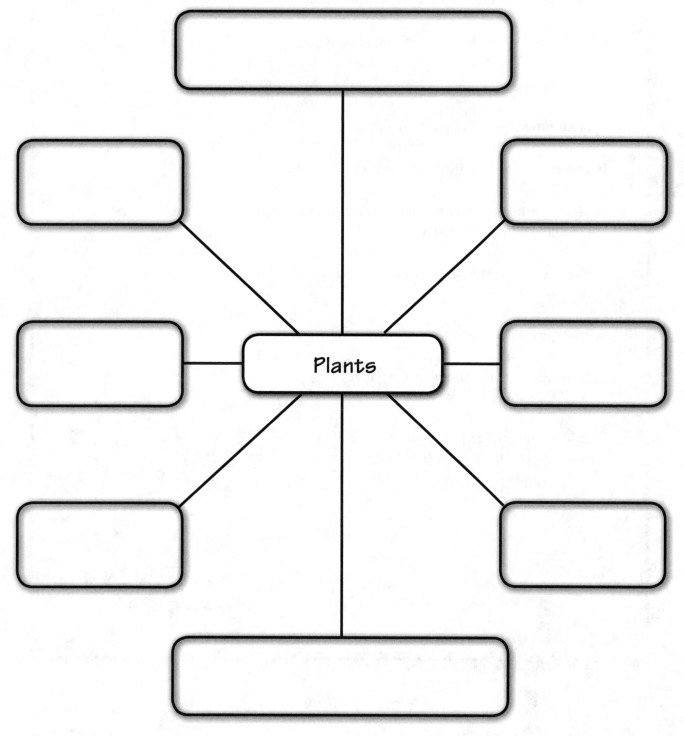

Plants

Vocabulary

1. **angiosperms**—flowering plants

2. **cellular respiration**—plant process that releases energy by breaking down glucose

3. **epidermis**—outer layer of cells on plant roots

4. **guard cells**—tiny cells on leaves that open and close the stomata

5. **gymnosperms**—cone-producing plants

6. **phloem**—cells that distribute sugar to the plants

7. **photosynthesis**—plant process that uses carbon dioxide, water, sunlight, and chlorophyll to produce glucose

8. **stoma** (*plural:* **stomata**)—tiny hole on leaves through which oxygen and carbon dioxide move

9. **transpiration**—the process by which water exits the stomata

10. **tropism**—a plant that grows toward or away from something in its environment

11. **xylem**—layer of cells that move nutrients from the root to other parts of plant

Plants

Brief #1: Vascular Plants

Most of the plants that you see all around you are vascular plants. Vascular plants can be trees with cones, flowering plants, fruit trees, and vegetables.

You have learned that the human body has a vascular system made of veins, capillaries, and arteries. These structures help people circulate blood and oxygen through their systems. Vascular plants also have a system that helps them to circulate through their structures the things that they need.

Focus

Vascular plants have parts that enable them to move water and nutrients through their system.

Vocabulary

1. epidermis
2. xylem
3. phloem
4. stoma
5. guard cells
6. transpiration

 ## Roots

The roots of vascular plants have very important jobs to do. First, they hold the plant in place. The roots of a vascular plant are like a ship's anchor. Without roots, vascular plants would simply blow away in storms or on a windy day.

But holding the plant in place is not the only job of the roots. It is the roots of the plant that draw in water and minerals from the soil into the plant.

The first place on the root that water and nutrients encounter is the epidermis. **The epidermis is an outer layer of cells on the roots.** They are covered in tiny hairs and these hairs help roots draw in the water and minerals that they need.

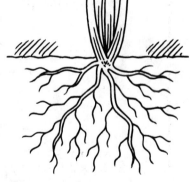

The next stop that water and nutrients make on their way through the plant is the xylem. **The xylem is a kind of plant escalator. The xylem is a layer of cells that move nutrients up from the roots to other parts of the plant. Finally, a type of plant cell called phloem distributes sugars produced in the leaves of the plant to all parts of the plant.**

 ## Stems

Like the roots of vascular plants, the stems also have more than one function. First, the stems of the plant help to support it. The stem of a plant is kind of like your spine. But plant stems also help to move and distribute water and nutrients around the plant.

Plant stems can be all shapes and sizes. Large trees and small flowering plants both have stems, but one is tall and has a thick brown trunk while the other is short, thin, and green. No matter the shape or size, stems all perform the same function in vascular plants.

Plants

Brief #1: Vascular Plants *(cont.)*

 Leaves

The job of the leaves on vascular plants is to produce a kind of sugar called glucose, which plants use as food.

You may not be able to see them, but there are tiny holes on each leaf. Each hole is called a stoma. **The stoma allows water and gases (oxygen and carbon dioxide) to pass in and out of the plant.** Around each little stoma there are guard cells. **The guard cells help to open and close the stoma.**

> ### Fast Fact
> The circumference of the trunk of General Sherman, the largest tree in the world, is 103 feet.

But what causes the guard cells to open and close the stoma? When sunlight hits a leaf, it causes the guard cells to fill with water. As the guard cell fills up, the water pushes the stoma open. Once the stoma opens up, gases in the air enter it and water passes out of it. **When the water leaves the stoma, that process is called transpiration.** This water evaporates.

As water leaves the stoma, it makes room for more water to enter the plants through the xylem and up through the roots. The stomata of most plants are open during the day and closed in the evening.

Leaf Structure

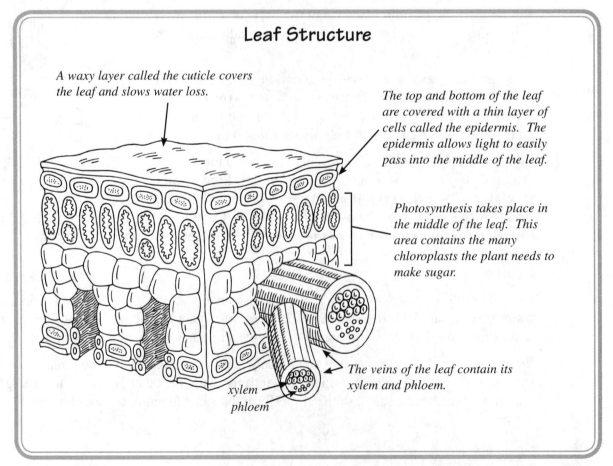

A waxy layer called the cuticle covers the leaf and slows water loss.

The top and bottom of the leaf are covered with a thin layer of cells called the epidermis. The epidermis allows light to easily pass into the middle of the leaf.

Photosynthesis takes place in the middle of the leaf. This area contains the many chloroplasts the plant needs to make sugar.

xylem
phloem

The veins of the leaf contain its xylem and phloem.

Plants

Brief #2: Photosynthesis

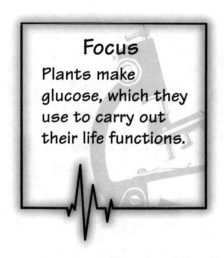

Focus

Plants make glucose, which they use to carry out their life functions.

Whether you're a plant or an animal, you have to consume energy in one form or another to survive. People can move around so they can gather the food that they need. But plants are very different. They are anchored in one place by their roots, so they have to make their own food in order to survive.

 Photosynthesis

Plant and animal cells have many things in common. But one thing that is very different between them is that plant cells contain chlorophyll. Chlorophyll is a substance that makes the leaves of plants green. It is also a very important ingredient in the production of food for plants. Without chlorophyll, plants would starve.

Photosynthesis is the process that plants use in order to make food. There is a simple equation that illustrates this process:

$$\text{carbon dioxide} + \text{water} \xrightarrow[\text{chlorophyll}]{\text{light energy}} \text{carbohydrates} + \text{oxygen}$$

What this equation is telling you is that plants take in carbon dioxide, water, and light energy from the sun, and they combine those things with chlorophyll. As a result of this combination, glucose and oxygen are produced.

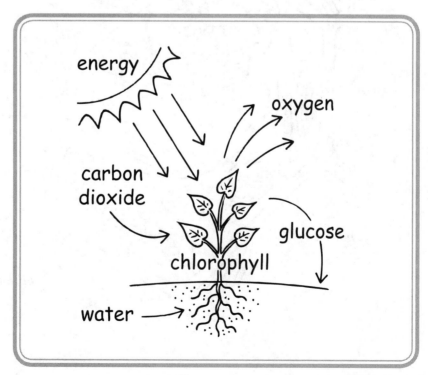

Plants

Brief #2: Photosynthesis *(cont.)*

 Photosynthesis *(cont.)*

You have probably noticed that when your parents go to the grocery store, they buy more food than is needed for one day. Much of this food is stored in closets and cabinets to be used when it is needed. Plants also can store food. They use a process called *cellular respiration* that enables them to change a surplus of glucose into other sugars and starches that can be stored and used when they're needed.

> ### Vocabulary
>
> 1. photosynthesis
>
> 2. cellular respiration

During cellular respiration, cells break down glucose, which releases its energy.

There is an equation that illustrates what happens during cellular respiration:

$$\textbf{glucose + oxygen} \longrightarrow \textbf{carbon dioxide + water + energy}$$

During this process, glucose is broken down into simpler substances in the cytoplasm of the cells. Oxygen in the cell moves these simpler substances from the cytoplasm to the mitochondria where oxygen continues to break the substances down into smaller and smaller materials. Finally, carbon dioxide and water are produced and energy is released into the organism through the mitochondria.

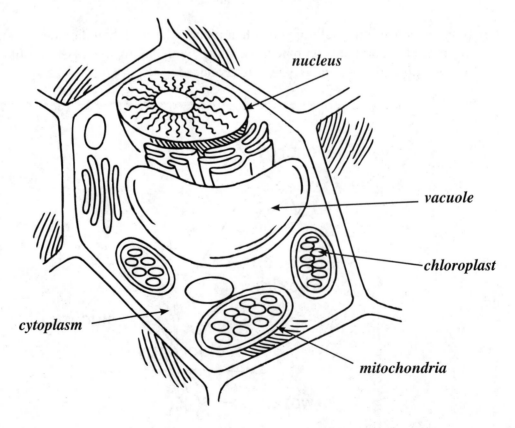

Plants

Brief #2: Photosynthesis (cont.)

 Interdependence of Plants and Animals

Plants and animals have a very special and important relationship. We need each other in order to survive on planet Earth. During the process of photosynthesis, plants produce oxygen as a byproduct. In other words, they release the oxygen into the atmosphere. Animals take in this oxygen as they inhale. When animals exhale, they release carbon dioxide into the atmosphere, which in turn is taken up by plants. This is called the *carbon dioxide-oxygen cycle*, and it is one of the reasons that life can exist on our planet. You will notice by examining the equations for the two processes that they are the opposites of each other.

$$\text{carbon dioxide} + \text{water} \xrightarrow[\text{chlorophyll}]{\text{light energy}} \text{glucose} + \text{oxygen}$$

$$\text{glucose} + \text{oxygen} \longrightarrow \text{carbon dioxide} + \text{water} + \text{energy}$$

Plants

Brief #3: Plant Growth

Vascular plants grow from seeds. Some seeds are produced in flowers. Other types of seeds are produced in cones. Different types of seeds need different types of things in order to grow.

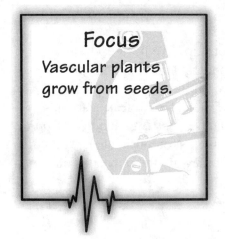

Focus
Vascular plants grow from seeds.

Vocabulary

1. angiosperms
2. gymnosperms
3. tropism

 Angiosperms

Angiosperms are flowering plants. Tulips, daisies, roses, cherry trees—any plant that produces a flower is an angiosperm. Most of the plants that exist on planet Earth are angiosperms.

Sometimes the seeds of angiosperms are found inside of fruit. For example, what we call the pit of an apricot is actually an apricot tree seed. And if you bite into an apple, you can see that the seeds for the apple tree are inside of the core.

The seeds of angiosperms are fertilized after pollination. Angiosperms rely on bees, birds, and other animals to carry the pollen to between plants.

 Gymnosperms

Gymnosperms are vascular plants that produce cones. The seeds of gymnosperms are located inside of these cones. Gymnosperms are called woody plants. Some types of gymnosperms are conifers. Conifers include redwood, pine, and spruce trees.

You may have noticed that sometimes cones are open and at other times they are closed. This has to do with the plant's reproduction.

Conifers produce male and female cones. The female cones contain the egg cells. The male cones produce pollen and sperm cells. The pollen is carried from the male cones to the female cones on the wind. After the female cones have been fertilized, they close up so the fertilized seeds can mature. When they are ready, the cone reopens and the seeds fall to the ground.

Plants

Brief #3: Plant Growth *(cont.)*

 ### Germination

Once the seeds of vascular plants enter the environment, they can begin to germinate. *Germination* means that the seed casing has broken open and the plant begins to sprout. Of course, the conditions in the environment have to be just right in order for a seed to germinate.

All seeds need the ground and air to be a particular temperature in order to geminate. Different seeds germinate in different temperatures. Seeds also need other things in order to geminate. They need a supply of oxygen and water. Once a seed germinates, the roots grow downward into the soil and the stem grows upward.

These vascular plants grow the same way other living things grow. The plants produce new cells at their roots. This causes the plant to get taller. It is kind of like the way that your hair grows. It doesn't grow from the ends or the middle, but from the root.

 ### Tropism

Just like animals, plants respond and change depending on what is happening in their environments. Some flowers open during the day and close their petals at night. The roots  of some plants grow in the direction of a water source. Sometimes, different chemicals can cause one part of a plant to grow at a different rate than another part of the same plant. This type of plant behavior is called tropism. **Tropism means that a plant is growing toward or away from something in its environment.**

Look at the table below to study different types of tropism. The prefixes (underlined) give a clue about the type of tropism being described.

Types of Tropism	Response to
<u>helio</u>tropism	sun
<u>hydro</u>tropism	water
<u>thermo</u>tropism	temperature
<u>gravito</u>tropism	gravity

Plants

Multiple-Choice Assessment

Name: _____ **Date:** _____

Directions: Read each question carefully. Fill in the correct answer circle.

1. What is one of the jobs of plant roots?

    Ⓐ to produce seeds

    Ⓑ to produce pollen

    Ⓒ to hold the plant in place

    Ⓓ to germinate the seeds

2. Nutrients and water are taken up by what part of the plants?

    Ⓐ petals

    Ⓑ roots

    Ⓒ sperm cells

    Ⓓ egg cells

3. What is the epidermis?

    Ⓐ outer layer of cells on plant roots

    Ⓑ outer layer of cells on stamen

    Ⓒ guard cells

    Ⓓ xylem cells

4. What covers the epidermis?

    Ⓐ tiny seeds

    Ⓑ hard covering

    Ⓒ tiny hairs

    Ⓓ none of these

5. What moves nutrients from the roots to other parts of the plant?

    Ⓐ epidermis

    Ⓑ stoma

    Ⓒ phloem

    Ⓓ xylem

Plants

Multiple-Choice Assessment *(cont.)*

6. What is the job of the phloem?

Ⓐ distribute sugars

Ⓑ distribute egg cells

Ⓒ to open and close the stoma

Ⓓ to open and close the guard cells

---

7. What helps to support the plant?

Ⓐ the stem

Ⓑ the bud

Ⓒ the stoma

Ⓓ the guard cells

---

8. Where is plant sugar produced?

Ⓐ the stem

Ⓑ the leaves

Ⓒ the roots

Ⓓ the xylem

---

9. How does oxygen and carbon dioxide get in and out of the plant?

Ⓐ the phloem

Ⓑ the stem

Ⓒ the stamen

Ⓓ the stoma

---

10. What is the job of the guard cells?

Ⓐ to open and closes the buds

Ⓑ to transport carbon dioxide to the leaves

Ⓒ the transport water from the roots to the leaves

Ⓓ to open and close the stoma

Plants

Multiple-Choice Assessment *(cont.)*

11. The process of transpiration happens when

    Ⓐ the guard cells open and close.

    Ⓑ the stoma opens and closes.

    Ⓒ water leaves the stoma.

    Ⓓ water enters the stoma.

---

12. What do plant cells have that animal cells do not have?

    Ⓐ chlorophyll

    Ⓑ nucleus

    Ⓒ cell wall

    Ⓓ all of these

---

13. What is photosynthesis?

    Ⓐ how plant release excess water

    Ⓑ how plants produce seeds

    Ⓒ how plants produce food

    Ⓓ how plants protect their roots

---

14. What are the raw materials that are used during photosynthesis?

    Ⓐ carbon dioxide, water, and oxygen

    Ⓑ carbon dioxide, water, light, and chlorophyll

    Ⓒ chlorophyll, carbon dioxide, light, and oxygen

    Ⓓ oxygen, chlorophyll and glucose

---

15. What is the food that plants produce?

    Ⓐ carbon

    Ⓑ oxygen

    Ⓒ minerals

    Ⓓ glucose

Plants

Multiple-Choice Assessment *(cont.)*

16. What process helps plants store food?

    Ⓐ cellular release

    Ⓑ cellular contraction

    Ⓒ cellular respiration

    Ⓓ cellular oxygenation

---

17. Which statement best describes the relationship between animals and plants?

    Ⓐ plants release carbon dioxide, animals breathe carbon dioxide

    Ⓑ animals breathe oxygen, plants release oxygen

    Ⓒ animals and plants breathe oxygen

    Ⓓ people exhale carbon dioxide and oxygen

---

18. What is an angiosperm?

    Ⓐ a cone producing plant

    Ⓑ a nonvascular plant

    Ⓒ a nonvascular tuber

    Ⓓ a flowering vascular plant

---

19. Where are the seeds located in gymnosperms?

    Ⓐ in the cones

    Ⓑ in the flowers

    Ⓒ in the fruit

    Ⓓ all of these

---

20. Which is an example of tropism?

    Ⓐ a germinating flower

    Ⓑ a closed cone

    Ⓒ a flower bending in the direction of the sun

    Ⓓ a rootless tree

Plants

Sentence-Completion Assessment

Name: _____ **Date:** _____

Directions: Read each statement. Fill in the word or words that best complete the sentence.

1. The _____ help to hold the plant in place.

2. _____ and _____ are taken up by the roots of the plant.

3. The _____ is an outer layer of cells on the plant roots.

4. Tiny _____ cover the epidermis.

5. A layer of cells called the _____ help to move nutrient from the roots to other parts of the plant.

6. Cells called _____ distribute sugars throughout the plant.

7. The _____ helps to support the plant.

8. Sugars are produced in the _____ of the plant.

9. Oxygen and carbon dioxide move in and out through the _____.

10. The _____ open and close the stomata.

Plants

Sentence-Completion Assessment *(cont.)*

11. When water leaves the stoma it is called _____.

12. _____ is what makes plants green.

13. Plants use the process of _____ to make food.

14. Plants use carbon dioxide, water, light and _____ in the production of food.

15. The food that plants produce is called _____ .

16. Plants store food using a process called _____ .

17. An _____ is a plant that produces flowers.

18. A _____ is a plant that produces cones.

19. When a seed begins to sprout it is called _____ .

20. _____ is when a plant moves or grows toward or away from something in the environment.

Plants

True-False Assessment

Name: _____ **Date:** _____

Directions: Read each statement carefully. If the statement is true, put a **T** on the line provided. If the statement is false, put an **F** on the line provided.

_____   **1.** Plant roots help to hold the plant in place.

_____   **2.** Nutrients are taken up by the petals of plants.

_____   **3.** The epidermis is located on the plant roots.

_____   **4.** The epidermis is covered in tiny scales.

_____   **5.** The xylem helps to convert sugar to energy.

_____   **6.** The phloem distributes sugars to the plant.

_____   **7.** The stem helps the plant in the process of photosynthesis.

_____   **8.** Sugar is produced in the stamen of the plant.

_____   **9.** Oxygen and carbon dioxide move in and out of the stomata.

_____   **10.** The guard cells distribute carbon dioxide to the plant.

Plants

True-False Assessment *(cont.)*

_____ **11.** During transpiration water leaves the stomata.

_____ **12.** Animal and plant cells have chlorophyll.

_____ **13.** Plants use the process of photosynthesis to produce food.

_____ **14.** During photosynthesis plants use oxygen and light to produce food.

_____ **15.** Plants produce glucose.

_____ **16.** Cellular respiration helps plants to store food.

_____ **17.** An angiosperm produces flowers.

_____ **18.** A gymnosperm produces flowers.

_____ **19.** The seeds of gymnosperm are located in the cones.

_____ **20.** Tropism means the fertilization of seeds.

Plants

Matching Assessment

Name: _____   **Date:** _____

Directions: Read the items in both lists below and on page 83 carefully. Choose an item from List B that best matches an item from List A. Write the corresponding letter from List B on the line. You will have some left over.

List A	List B
_____ **1.** job of roots	**A.** minerals
_____ **2.** epidermis	**B.** tiny leaf holes
_____ **3.** epidermis covering	**C.** cone maker
_____ **4.** xylem	**D.** nutrient mover
_____ **5.** phloem	**E.** closed
_____ **6.** stem job	**F.** chlorophyll
_____ **7.** where sugar is made	**G.** flowering plant
_____ **8.** stomata	**H.** gravity
_____ **9.** guard cells	**I.** leaves
_____ **10.** transpiration	**J.** germination
_____ **11.** plants cells only	**K.** root cells
_____ **12.** food making process	**L.** open and close stomata

GO

Plants

Matching Assessment *(cont.)*

List A	List B
_____ **13.** plant food	**M.** tiny hairs
_____ **14.** ingredients for plant food	**N.** food storage
_____ **15.** cellular respiration	**O.** environmental response
_____ **16.** angiosperm	**P.** sugar distributor
_____ **17.** gymnosperm	**Q.** draw in water and nutrients
_____ **18.** tropism	**R.** plant support
_____ **19.** sprouting seed	**S.** water exits leaves
_____ **20.** fertilized cone	**T.** carbon dioxide, water, light energy, chlorophyll
	U. pollination
	V. glucose
	W. photosynthesis

STOP

Plants

Graphic Assessment

Name: _____   **Date:** _____

Directions: Locate and label the following parts of the leaf below: *cuticle, epidermis, xylem,* and *phloem.* Also label the area in the leaf where photosynthesis takes place.

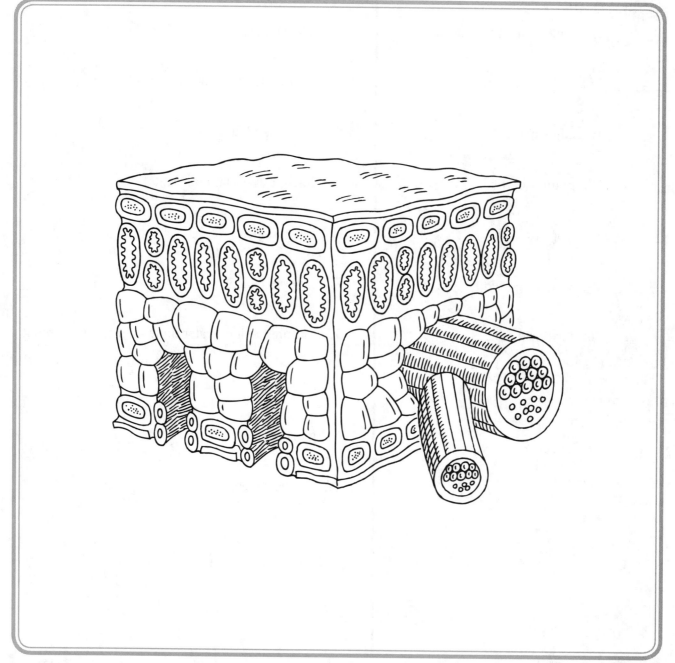

Plants

Short-Response Assessment

Name: _____ **Date:** _____

Directions: Read each question carefully. Write a short response of a few sentences to each question.

1. Describe the processes of photosynthesis and cellular respiration. Why are these called opposite processes?

_____

_____

_____

_____

_____

2. What is tropism? Provide examples.

_____

_____

_____

_____

_____

3. Explain how vascular plants grow. Describe how both flowering plants and cone-producing plants go about this process.

_____

_____

_____

_____

4. Explain what is meant by plant and animal interdependence. What would happen to animals in a world without plants?

_____

_____

_____

_____

STOP

Plate Tectonics

Teacher Materials

 Teacher Preparation

Before you begin this unit, photocopy and distribute the following to students:

- Student Introduction (page 89)
- Unit Vocabulary (page 90)
- Student Briefs (pages 91–97)
- Appropriate Assessments (pages 98–109)

 Key Unit Concepts

- The Earth is made up of the *crust, mantle,* and *core*.
- The *lithosphere* is the crust and upper mantle.
- The lithosphere is made of giant plates that float on top of the lower mantle.
- A *scientific theory* is an idea that attempts to explain something observed.
- *Empirical evidence* is evidence that can be perceived by one of the five senses.
- *Continental drift* explains why the continents are located where they are located.
- *Pangaea* is the name of the super continent that existed before the continents broke apart.
- *Sea floor spreading* explains how the continents broke apart and moved to their current locations.
- *Plate tectonics* is the study of Earth's plates.
- The Earth's plates behave differently at the boundaries.
- *Earthquakes* and *volcanoes* are caused by the action of the Earth's plates.
- The *focus* and *epicenter* describe different features of an earthquake.
- Technology can be used to make predictions about earthquakes and volcanoes.
- Volcanoes and earthquakes change the land.

 Discussion Topics

- Have students brainstorm a list of natural physical features of the area in which they live.
- Have students discuss the importance of proving scientific theories with empirical evidence.

See "Generic Strategies and Activities" on pages 8 and 9 for additional strategies useful to presenting this unit.

Plate Tectonics

Activities

 Brief #1: The Layers of the Earth

- **Make a Model:** Make a clay model that illustrates the layers of the Earth.

  Supplies: Five different colors of clay, toothpicks, small sticky labels, knife

  Procedure: Select a different color for each layer of the Earth: inner core, outer core, lower mantle, upper mantle, and crust. Next, make a small clay ball to represent the inner core. Cover the clay core in another color of clay to represent the outer core. Continue this process to make the rest of the layers of the Earth. When your model is finished, use a sharp knife to carefully cut your model in half. When you do this, it will expose the various layers that you created. Make small labels with toothpicks and sticky labels to name the layers.

- **Make a Model:** Make a Styrofoam model of the Earth's major tectonic plates.

  Supplies: large Styrofoam board, glue, craft knife, pencil, paste, different colors of construction paper, scissors, toothpicks, sticky labels, map of Earth's major tectonic plates

  Procedure: Use a pencil to trace the major plates onto the Styrofoam. Use the craft knife to cut out the plates. Next, draw the major landmasses on different colors of construction paper. Cut these landmasses out and paste them onto the correct plates. Use the toothpicks and sticky labels to create labels and stick them into the Styrofoam.

  Key Words: *layers of Earth, Earth's major tectonic plates*

 Brief #2: Continental Drift

- **Write a Rap, Song, or Poem:** Write a poem, song, or rap that explains scientific theory and empirical evidence.

- **Write and Perform an Interview:** Research the life of Alfred Wegener, the scientist who developed the theory of continental drift. Write five interview questions and answers. Then act out the interview for classmates—one person playing Wegener, the other playing the interviewer.

- **Choreograph a Dance Routine:** Create a dance routine that illustrates how sea-floor spreading occurs. Select music to accompany your routine that you think in some way helps to show this process.

  Key Words: *Alfred Wegener, continental drift, sea-floor spreading*

 Brief #3: The Theory of Plate Tectonics

- **Make an Informational Poster:** Make an informational poster that illustrates and explains transform, divergent, and convergent boundaries.

- **Make a Table:** Make a data table that tells what the Earth's major tectonic plates are and how quickly they are moving each year.

Plate Tectonics

Activities (cont.)

 ### Brief #3: The Theory of Plate Tectonics (cont.)

- **Write a Research Brief:** Conduct research to discover the landforms that have been created at the points of plate boundaries. (For example, the Great Rift Valley is a consequence of plates moving away from each other.) Create a short brief that describes some of these landforms. You may include illustrations with your brief.

   Key Words: *tectonic plate boundaries, tectonic plates, landforms*

 ### Brief #4: Earthquakes and Volcanoes

- **Build a Shake Table:** A shake table is a simple model that allows students to simulate how seismic activity can damage structures.

   Supplies: one large cardboard box, marbles, a piece of cardboard cut in the same shape of the box and able to fit easily inside of the box, a variety of things that student can build small structures from (toothpicks, marshmallows, gumdrops, string, clay, etc.)

   Procedure: Place marbles in the bottom of the cardboard box. Next, place the piece of cardboard on top of the marbles. Have students build various structures from the given supplies and then put them on top of the cardboard. Instruct them to shake the box for varying lengths of times and at various intensities to see how their structures hold up. After students have had an opportunity to test 3–4 structures, have them write a short brief that explains what they discovered.

- **Write a Narrative:** Ask students to pretend that they witnessed the San Francisco earthquake of 1906. Have them research and then write a one-page, first-person account of their experience.

- **Make an Information Poster:** Have students make an informational poster about volcano safety. The poster should contain information on what to do before, during, and after a volcanic eruption.

   Key Words: *1906 San Francisco earthquake, volcano safety*

 ### Internet Resources

- *http://earthquake.usgs.gov/regional/neic/index.php* — the official website of the U.S. Geological Survey; includes up-to-date information about latest earthquakes

- *http://www.archives.gov/exhibits/sf-earthquake-and-fire/* — a National Archives site about the 1906 San Francisco earthquake

- *http://www.mnh.si.edu/earth/main_frames.html* — a site from National Museum of Natural History called "The Dynamic Earth"

Plate Tectonics

Student Introduction: Plate Tectonics Word Web

Name: _____ **Date:** _____

Directions: Use this word web to help you brainstorm the characteristics of plate tectonics.

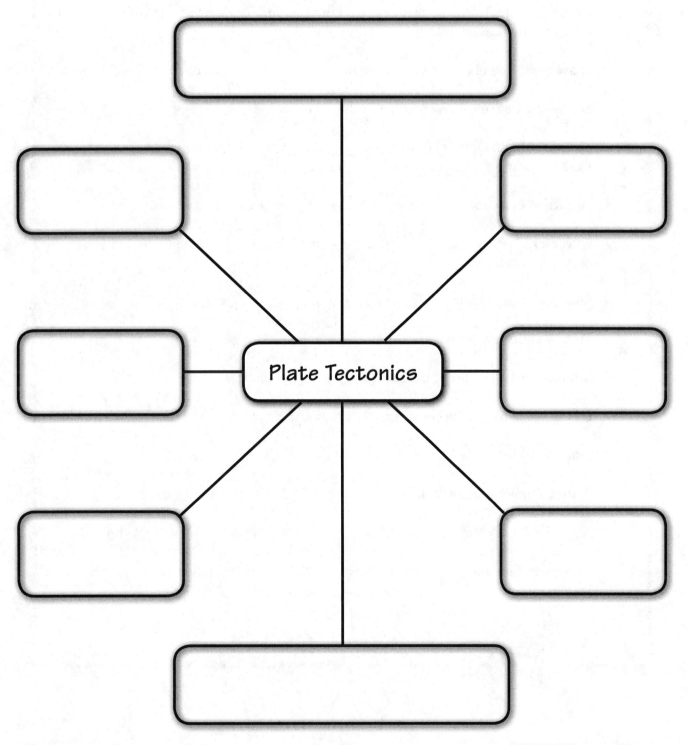

Plate Tectonics

Vocabulary

1. **core**—the iron center of the Earth

2. **continental drift**—theory that explains how the Earth's continents came to be in their present locations

3. **convergent boundary**—place where two of the Earth's plates crash into each other

4. **crust**—the outermost layer of the Earth

5. **divergent boundary**—place where two of the Earth's plates are spreading away from one another

6. **empirical evidence**—evidence that can be observed by the five senses

7. **epicenter**—the area on the Earth's crust located directly above the focus of an earthquake

8. **fault**—a huge crack in the crust of the Earth

9. **focus**—place beneath the ground where an earthquake begins

10. **lithosphere**—the crust of the Earth and the upper mantle

11. **mantle**—the part of the Earth directly beneath the crust

12. **plate boundary**—the place where two of the Earth's plates meet

13. **plate tectonics**—study of the Earth's plates and the features they produce

14. **scientific theory**—an idea that gives an explanation of something that is observed

15. **transform boundary**—place where two of the Earth's plates slide past each other

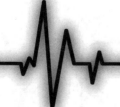

Plate Tectonics

Brief #1: The Layers of the Earth

Focus

The Earth is made up of three distinct layers.

When you look at the surface of the Earth, you can see that it is not just a large piece of flat land. The Earth is full of high mountains, low valleys, canyons, cracks, and slopes. The form of the land has many shapes and sizes.

The Earth is made up of three different layers:

✓ the crust
✓ the mantle
✓ the core

Vocabulary

1. crust
2. mantle
3. core
4. lithosphere

 ### The Crust

The outermost layer of the Earth is called the crust. The crust is where life on Earth exists. The crust of the Earth is made of rock and soil. In addition, there are other kinds of elements—like iron, sodium, and silicon—in the Earth's crust.

The thickness of the crust of the Earth is different in different places. For example, the part of the crust beneath the ocean is about six and a half miles thick. The part that is dry land is about 25 miles thick. The crust is only a small part of the material that makes up the planet.

The Mantle

The part of the Earth located beneath the crust is called the mantle. The mantle is the largest part of the planet. The part of the mantle just beneath the crust is made of solid rock. But the deeper you go in the mantle, the hotter it becomes. It is so hot that the inner part of the mantle is made up of molten rock that flows inside of the Earth. The mantle of the Earth is about 1,800 miles thick.

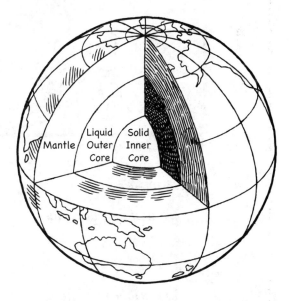

 ### The Core

The core is at the center of the Earth.
The core of the Earth has a radius of about 758 miles. Its temperature is about 7,000 degrees Celsius. The inner part of the Earth's core is solid iron. The outer part of the core is liquid iron and nickel.

Plate Tectonics

Brief #1: The Layers of the Earth *(cont.)*

 ### The Lithosphere

The crust of the Earth is like a giant shell. But it is not a single solid piece of shell. **The crust of the Earth and the upper mantle is called the lithosphere.** This lithosphere is really a collection of large pieces of solid rock, not that different from the pieces of a puzzle. These giant pieces of crust and mantle are called plates. You can see the Earth's plates on the map below.

The plates are not the same size or shape as the continents. In fact, whole continents and parts of vast oceans can rest on top of a single plate. The lithosphere floats on top of the liquid part of the mantle.

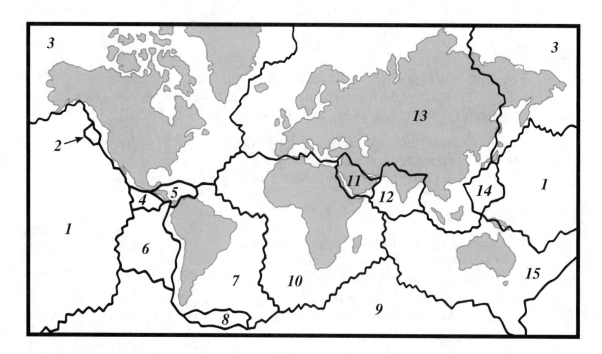

1. Pacific Plate	9. Antarctic Plate
2. Juan de Fuca Plate	10. African Plate
3. North American Plate	11. Arabian Plate
4. Cocos Plate	12. Indian Plate
5. Caribbean Plate	13. Eurasian Plate
6. Nazca Plate	14. Philippine Plate
7. South American Plate	15. Indo-Australian Plate
8. Scotia Plate	

Plate Tectonics

Brief #2: Continental Drift

Focus

Continental drift explains the location of the continents.

A scientific theory is an idea or concept that gives an explanation for something observed. Here is an example: suppose one day on your way home from school you observed a large tree laying across the middle of your street. Naturally, you would ask how the tree got there.

Next, you might develop a theory based on what you currently know about the way the world works to explain how the tree got there. One theory may be that the tree fell. Another theory may be that it was cut down.

After you have developed a theory, you will have to set about gathering evidence that will either prove or disprove your theory. It is important to remember that when you test a scientific theory, the evidence must be empirical. **Empirical evidence is evidence that can be observed by your five senses.**

Vocabulary

1. scientific theory

2. empirical evidence

3. continental drift

Alfred Wegener

Around 1912, a German geologist named Alfred Wegener developed a theory called continental drift. **Continental drift is a theory that explains how the Earth's continents came to be in their current locations.** If you are like Wegener, you probably have noticed that the continents look like giant puzzle pieces. Wegener's theory explains why that is.

Wegener believed that at one time, millions and millions of years ago, all of the continents were joined together in one giant piece. This super continent is known as Pangaea. Wegener believed that the shape of the continents was one piece of empirical evidence that supported his theory.

Other empirical evidence included plant and animal fossils. The fossils showed that many of the same types of plants and animals lived along the eastern coast of South America and the western coast of Africa. These fossils suggested that at one time these plants and animals lived together in the same area when the continents were joined together.

Even though the shape of the continents and the fossil record were two strong pieces of evidence to support Wegener's theory, it still wasn't enough to prove it. Wegener's theory did not explain how the continents moved.

Plate Tectonics

Brief #2: Continental Drift *(cont.)*

 ### Sea-Floor Spreading

It was a not until the 1960s—about 50 years after Alfred Wegener proposed his theory of continental drift—that new evidence surfaced that could explain how the continents may have broken apart and drifted to their present locations. Scientists discovered that the ocean floor had long underwater mountain chains and deep trenches. They wondered how those trenches and mountains got there.

It was discovered that hot magma from the Earth's mantle pushes up through the part of the Earth's crust that is beneath the ocean. As the magma flows up and out, it cools off and forms new crust. This new crust pushes the old crust aside. This action causes the sea floor to spread apart, which in turn pushes the continents apart.

World Maps

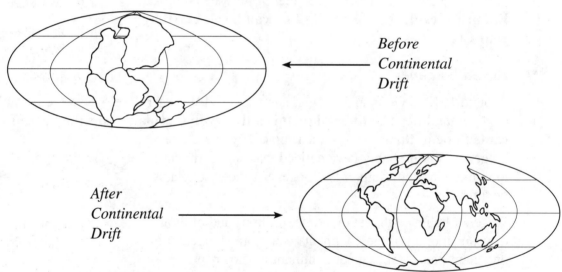

Before Continental Drift

After Continental Drift

 ### Earth's Magnetic Field

Another piece of empirical evidence to support the theory of continental drift involves the Earth's magnetic field. The current of Earth's magnetic field can either run from north to south or in the opposite direction, from south to north. Scientists discovered that about every 500,000 years, Earth's magnetic field reverses. There is evidence of this on the ocean floor.

When the magnetic field reverses, all of the new rocks that form from lava at that time have a certain type of magnetic pattern. When scientists examined the parts of the ocean floor, they saw this reversing pattern on the ocean floor. This proved that the sea-floor spread caused the continents to drift apart over the course of millions of years.

Plate Tectonics

Brief #3: The Theory of Plate Tectonics

You have read earlier in the unit that the Earth's lithosphere is made up of moving plates. There are about 20 of these plates on our planet. Because the plates are resting on top of the molten part of the mantle, they are always moving. Of course, they move slowly and very little, but they move in all different directions.

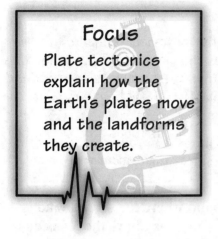

Focus

Plate tectonics explain how the Earth's plates move and the landforms they create.

As the plates move, they create the features that we can see on the crust of the Earth. Things like canyons, mountains, and valleys are a result of the constantly moving plates. **The study of the Earth's plates and the features they produce is called plate tectonics.**

Vocabulary

1. plate tectonics
2. plate boundary
3. transform boundary
4. divergent boundary
5. convergent boundary
6. fault

Plate Boundaries

A plate boundary is the place where two of the Earth's plates meet. The plates can move away from each other, move towards each other, or slide past each other. There are three different types of plate boundaries:

✓ **A transform boundary is when two plates slide past each other.**

✓ **A divergent boundary is when two plates move away from each other.**

✓ **A convergent boundary is when two plates crash into each other.**

At transform boundaries, faults are created. **A fault is a huge break in the crust of the Earth.** The San Andreas Fault in California is an example of a transform boundary. At divergent boundaries, large valleys can be formed. The Great Rift Valley in Africa is an example of a spreading valley. At convergent boundaries, mountain ranges can be produced. The Andes Mountains in South America is an example of a convergent boundary.

Scientists use GPS (global positioning system) satellites to map the Earth's plates and to measure how the plates are moving relative to one another. Using this kind of technology, they can make predictions about where the continents may be in 100 years to 1,000 years— or even one million years from now! Some of the Earth's plates are moving toward each other at a rate of about four inches per year, and others are moving away from each other. Some scientists say that millions of years in the future, the Earth's continents could come together once again and reform something similar to the ancient Pangaea.

Plate Tectonics

Brief #4: Earthquakes and Volcanoes

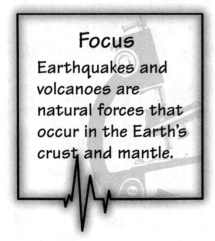

Focus

Earthquakes and volcanoes are natural forces that occur in the Earth's crust and mantle.

 Earthquakes

Earthquakes are caused by the movement of the Earth's tectonic plates. When plates slide past each other, bump into each other, or move away from each other, pressure builds up in the Earth's crust.

Eventually, that pressure will be released in the form of an earthquake.

Vocabulary

1. focus
2. epicenter

The place beneath the ground where the earthquake begins is called the focus. The area above the focus on the crust of the Earth is called the epicenter.

When an earthquake happens, the energy from it is carried out away from the epicenter. The seismic waves can make the ground move back and forth. Other seismic waves can make the ground move up and down, like a wave in the ocean.

Earthquake strength is measured in magnitude on the Richter scale. The scale measures magnitude from 1 to 10. Each increase of one number on the Richter scale means that the earthquake releases about 31 times more energy. So an earthquake with a magnitude of 7.0 is 31 times more powerful than an earthquake with a magnitude of 6.0.

 Volcano

Volcanoes are openings in the surface of the Earth's plates where hot magma rises and overflows out onto the crust of the Earth. Many volcanoes occur at the boundaries of plates. For example, as convergent plates crash into each other, one can slide underneath the other. That crust can melt and become magma, which can then explode through the crust as a volcano. (See page 97 for a diagram of a volcano's parts.)

 Earthquake and Volcano Safety

Even though earthquakes and volcanoes are natural events, they can cause a lot of damage. Earthquakes can destroy whole cities, and the hot lava that flows from volcanoes can destroy all living things in its path.

Fortunately, there are tools that scientists can use to better our understanding about when these natural events may happen. Seismographs are instruments that can detect tremors in the ground. A tiltmeter can show changes in the slope of land. Tremors and a change in the land can be an indication of a volcano or an earthquake.

Plate Tectonics

Brief #4: Earthquakes and Volcanoes (cont.)

 Parts of a Volcano

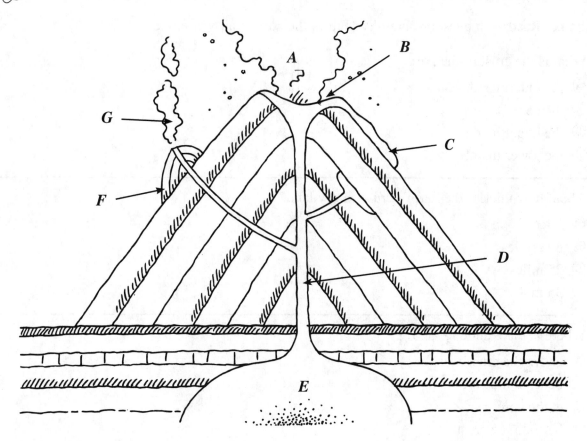

A. **ash cloud:** *bits of rock that are spewed out from the volcano upon eruption*

B. **crater:** *bowl-shaped depression at the top of a volcano*

C. **lava flow:** *magma that has erupted out of the volcano and is flowing down the side*

D. **conduit:** *a pipe that leads from the reservoir to the crater*

E. **magma reservoir:** *area where a large amount of magma is located*

F. **parasitic cone:** *a smaller cone that forms on the side of a volcano*

G. **side vent:** *an opening on the side of a volcano out of which lava flows*

Plate Tectonics

Multiple-Choice Assessment

Name: _____   **Date:** _____

Directions: Read each question carefully. Fill in the correct answer circle.

1. What is the crust of the Earth?

    Ⓐ the outermost layer

    Ⓑ the core

    Ⓒ the upper mantle

    Ⓓ the lower mantle

2. About how thick is the Earth's crust on dry land?

    Ⓐ 2 feet

    Ⓑ 6 ½ miles

    Ⓒ 25 miles

    Ⓓ 35 miles

3. Where is the mantle located?

    Ⓐ above the crust

    Ⓑ beneath the core

    Ⓒ at the core

    Ⓓ beneath the crust

4. What is the center of the Earth called?

    Ⓐ the mantle

    Ⓑ the lower mantle

    Ⓒ the core

    Ⓓ the magma

5. What form is the Earth's mantle?

    Ⓐ solid

    Ⓑ liquid

    Ⓒ gaseous

    Ⓓ liquid and solid

Plate Tectonics

Multiple-Choice Assessment *(cont.)*

6. What is the Earth's inner core made of?

   Ⓐ liquid rock

   Ⓑ liquid iron

   Ⓒ solid iron

   Ⓓ liquid nickel

---

7. What is the lithosphere?

   Ⓐ the crust and the upper mantle

   Ⓑ the crust and the lower mantle

   Ⓒ the plates

   Ⓓ the upper core and lower mantle

---

8. What is a scientific theory?

   Ⓐ a belief based on something a person thinks

   Ⓑ an idea that provides an explanation for something observed

   Ⓒ an equation

   Ⓓ a formula

---

9. Empirical evidence is evidence that can be

   Ⓐ seen and heard.

   Ⓑ touched and tasted.

   Ⓒ smelled.

   Ⓓ all of these

---

10. What is Pangaea?

    Ⓐ a map of the Earth

    Ⓑ an ancient super continent

    Ⓒ a theory

    Ⓓ empirical evidence

Plate Tectonics

Multiple-Choice Assessment *(cont.)*

11. What evidence did Wegener have that supported his theory of continental drift?

Ⓐ sea-floor spreading

Ⓑ images from radio GPS

Ⓒ old maps

Ⓓ fossils

---

12. Which of the following best explains sea-floor spreading?

Ⓐ tectonic plates push the sea floor up

Ⓑ tectonic plates collapse under their own weight

Ⓒ underwater volcanoes produce new crust

Ⓓ newly formed crust on the ocean floor pushes old crust apart

---

13. What happens to the Earth's magnetic field about every 500,000 years?

Ⓐ It gets stronger.

Ⓑ It reverses.

Ⓒ It stops.

Ⓓ all of these

---

14. What is the area where plates meet called?

Ⓐ a plate fault

Ⓑ a focus

Ⓒ an epicenter

Ⓓ a plate boundary

---

15. What happens at a divergent boundary?

Ⓐ plates collide

Ⓑ plates slide past one another

Ⓒ plates melt

Ⓓ plates move away from each other

Plate Tectonics

Multiple-Choice Assessment *(cont.)*

16. Plates slide past each other at a

Ⓐ divergent boundary.

Ⓑ a transform boundary.

Ⓒ a convergent boundary.

Ⓓ a vent.

---

17. What is a fault?

Ⓐ a huge volcano

Ⓑ a plate

Ⓒ a huge break in the crust of the Earth

Ⓓ a huge break in the mantle of the Earth

---

18. What is a parasitic cone?

Ⓐ a type of tectonic plate

Ⓑ a type of ash cloud

Ⓒ a structure formed on the side of a volcano

Ⓓ a bowl-shaped depression

---

19. Why do volcanoes often form at plate boundaries?

Ⓐ Plates create huge seismic waves.

Ⓑ Plates can slide beneath each other.

Ⓒ Plates are explosive.

Ⓓ none of these

---

20. Where would you find the crater of a volcano?

Ⓐ at the top

Ⓑ at the bottom

Ⓒ on the basalt plane

Ⓓ near the geyser

Plate Tectonics

Sentence-Completion Assessment

Name: _____   **Date:** _____

Directions: Read each statement. Fill in the word or words that best complete the sentence.

1. The outermost layer of the Earth is called the _____ .

2. The crust of the Earth located on dry land is about _____ miles thick.

3. The _____ is located directly beneath the crust.

4. The center of the Earth is called the _____ .

5. The Earth's mantle is both a solid and a _____ .

6. The inner core of the Earth is made of solid _____ .

7. The _____ is made up of the crust and the upper mantle.

8. An idea that provides an explanation for an observation is called a _____

    _____ .

9. Evidence that can be observed by your five senses is called _____ .

10. _____ was an ancient super continent.

Plate Tectonics

Sentence-Completion Assessment *(cont.)*

11. Wegener used fossils to help to support his theory of _____ .

12. Newly formed crust on the ocean floor that pushes old crust out of the way is called

_____ .

13. The Earth's _____ reverses about every 500,000 years.

14. The area where Earth's plates meet is called the _____ .

15. Plates move away from each other at a _____ boundary.

16. Plates slide past each other at a _____ boundary.

17. A huge crack in the Earth's crust is called a _____ .

18. A _____ is a smaller structure formed on the side of a volcano.

19. An _____ is formed when tiny bits of rock spew during a volcanic eruption.

20. A volcano's crater is located at the _____ .

Plate Tectonics

True-False Assessment

Name: _____ **Date:** _____

Directions: Read each statement carefully. If the statement is true, put a **T** on the line provided. If the statement is false, put an **F** on the line provided.

_____ **1.** The crust of the Earth is the outermost layer.

_____ **2.** The Earth's crust on dry land is about 25 miles thick.

_____ **3.** The mantle is located at the center of the Earth.

_____ **4.** The center of the Earth is called the crust.

_____ **5.** The Earth's mantle is both liquid and solid.

_____ **6.** The Earth's inner core is made of solid iron.

_____ **7.** The lithosphere is the mantle of the Earth.

_____ **8.** A scientific theory is an explanation for something observed.

_____ **9.** Beliefs are the same as empirical evidence.

_____ **10.** Pangaea is an ancient super continent

GO

Plate Tectonics

True-False Assessment *(cont.)*

_____ **11.** Wegener had fossil evidence to support his continental drift theory.

_____ **12.** Newly formed crust that pushes old crust apart at the bottom of the ocean is called sea-floor spreading.

_____ **13.** The Earth's magnetic field vanishes every 500,000 years.

_____ **14.** The Earth's plates meet at plate boundaries.

_____ **15.** The Earth's plates move past one another at divergent boundaries.

_____ **16.** The Earth's plates move apart at divergent boundaries.

_____ **17.** A huge crack in the crust of the Earth is called a fault.

_____ **18.** A conduit is a volcanic ash cloud.

_____ **19.** Volcanoes often form at plate boundaries because the boundaries are made of magma.

_____ **20.** The crater of a volcano is located at the top.

Plate Tectonics

Matching Assessment

Name: _____ **Date:** _____

Directions: Read the items in both lists below and on page 107 carefully. Choose an item from List B that best matches an item from List A. Write the corresponding letter from List B on the line. You will have some left over.

List A	List B
_____ 1. crust	**A.** side vent
_____ 2. core	**B.** liquid iron and nickel
_____ 3. upper mantle	**C.** fault
_____ 4. lower mantle	**D.** 758 miles
_____ 5. lithosphere	**E.** made of magma
_____ 6. core radius	**F.** Wegner theory
_____ 7. core temperature	**G.** top
_____ 8. empirical evidence	**H.** separating plates
_____ 9. continental drift	**I.** 7,000 degrees Celsius
_____ 10. Pangaea	**J.** directly beneath crust
_____ 11. reverses every 500,000 years	**K.** convergent boundary
_____ 12. plate tectonics	**L.** sliding plates

Plate Tectonics

Matching Assessment *(cont.)*

List A	List B
_____ **13.** transform boundary	**M.** super continent
_____ **14.** divergent boundary	**N.** 25 miles
_____ **15.** huge crack in Earth	**O.** magnetic field
_____ **16.** crater	**P.** sea-floor spreading
_____ **17.** location of volcano crater	**Q.** bowl-shaped depression
_____ **18.** crust thickness	**R.** outermost layer
_____ **19.** inner core material	**S.** center of Earth
_____ **20.** outer core material	**T.** crust and upper mantle
	U. study of Earth's plates
	V. observed by senses
	W. solid iron
	X. liquid iron

STOP

Plate Tectonics

Graphic Assessment

Name: _____   **Date:** _____

Directions: Locate and label the following parts of the volcano below: *ash cloud, crater, lava flow, conduit, magma reservoir, parasitic cone,* and *side vent.*

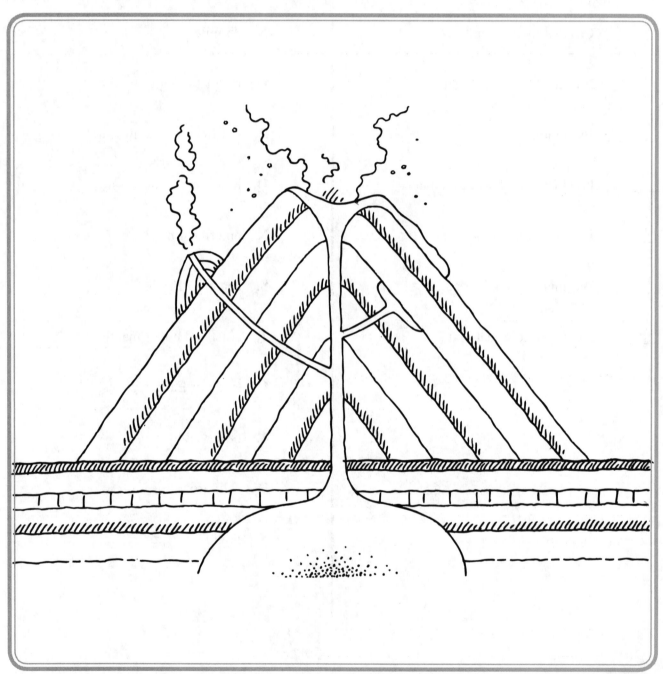

Plate Tectonics

Short-Response Assessment

Name: _____ **Date:** _____

Directions: Read each question carefully. Write a short response of a few sentences to each question.

1. Explain Wegener's theory of continental drift. What empirical evidence did he have to support his theory? What question did his theory answer? What question did his theory leave unanswered?

   _____

   _____

   _____

   _____

2. What is meant by *empirical evidence*? Why is empirical evidence a necessity in scientific investigation?

   _____

   _____

   _____

   _____

   _____

3. What is the lithosphere? Explain the dynamics of the lithosphere.

   _____

   _____

   _____

   _____

4. Describe how sea-floor spreading moves tectonic plates.

   _____

   _____

   _____

   _____

Matter

Teacher Materials

 Teacher Preparation

Before you begin this unit, photocopy and distribute the following to students:

- Student Introduction (page 113)
- Unit Vocabulary (page 114)
- Student Briefs (pages 115–122)*
- Appropriate Assessments (pages 123–134)

* *A complete Periodic Table of Elements is featured on page 117. Direct students to use colored pencils to color the gases blue, the solids yellow, the liquids green, and the elements not found in nature red. Color the zinc and silicon blocks yellow.*

 Key Unit Concepts

- Atoms are the smallest pieces of matter on Earth.
- Everything is made of atoms.
- An *electron-cloud model* is a model of atomic structure.
- *Elements* are pure substances that are made up of a single type of atom.
- There are 100 natural elements present on Earth.
- Elements can be metals, nonmetals or metalloids.
- The *Periodic Table of Elements* shows all of the elements that are present on Earth.
- A *compound* is a substance made of two or more atoms that are chemically bonded.
- All compounds have formulas.
- *Mixtures* and *solutions* are not chemically bonded.
- Solutions are mixtures in which substances are dissolved.
- *Solvent, solute, concentration,* and *solubility* define and describe the constituent parts of solutions.
- *Acids* and *bases* are types of solutions.
- The *pH scale* measures the strength of acids and bases.

 Discussion Topics

- Brainstorm a list of elements. How are these elements used? Where would you most likely find them?
- Aside from the pH scale and the periodic table, have students brainstorm some other tables that are used in science.

See "Generic Strategies and Activities" on pages 8 and 9 for additional strategies useful to presenting this unit.

Matter

Activities

 Brief #1: Atoms

- **Make an Illustrated Timeline:** Have students research the development of atomic theory and the contributions and discoveries of Democritus, John Dalton, Joseph John Thomson, Ernest Rutherford, Neils Bohr, and Erwin Schrödinger. Ask each student to make an illustrated timeline that depicts important developments in atomic theory.

- **Use a Venn diagram:** Ask students to select two different types of atoms. Using a Venn diagram, have them compare and contrast the atoms. As an example, students may want to compare and contrast the krypton atom with the gold atom.

- **Make an Electron-cloud model:** Have students select one atom. Using a large piece of poster board and markers, draw an electron-cloud model of that atom.

  Key Words: *Democritus, John Dalton, Joseph John Thomson, Ernest Rutherford, Neils Bohr, Erwin Schrödinger, elements, electron-cloud model*

 Brief #2: Elements

- **Play "Atomic Number Math":** Have students use the atomic numbers of the elements and find the answer using mental math: mercury + thallium – nitrogen + potassium = (the answer is 173). Have students make up several problems of their own to share with classmates.

- **Play "What Element Am I?":** Assign partner groups. Have each student provide clues about a particular element and have the other student in the pair name the element. Here is an example: I am a noble gas with 18 protons. (Answer: argon)

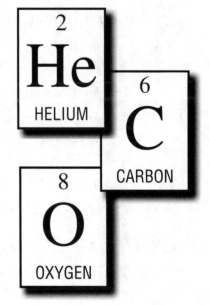

- **Play "Periodic Table Mash-Up":** Using 8½" x 11" pieces of cardboard, have students make a large deck of element cards from the periodic table. On one side of the card, have students write the atomic number and the chemical symbol. Using separate pieces of cardboard or paper, have students create one label for each element. The label should have the full name of the element. Scramble the cards on the floor. Have students arrange the cards in the correct order. After they have been arranged, have them match the element name with the correct atomic number and symbol.

  Key Words: *elements, periodic table*

Matter

Activities *(cont.)*

 Brief #3: Compounds, Mixtures, and Solutions

- **Make a Solution:** Add one teaspoonful of sugar to an 8-ounce glass of water. Stir. Observe how the sugar dissolves into the water to create a solution.

- **Make a Mixture:** Take a walk around your school or in the school playground. Collect five natural materials and put them in a small plastic baggie. Bring the baggie back to the classroom and swap with a classmate. Identify the different materials in the mixture.

- **Demonstrate a Chemical Bond:** Have students use themselves to make a moving model of how the electrons move in a chemical bond.

- **Make an Informational Poster:** Using poster board and colorful markers, create a poster that shows five acids and five bases that are encountered in everyday life. Make sure to label them and tell what they are used for.

- **Play Compound Detective:** Gather five packaged items that contain labels. Make a list of the active ingredients in these products and then research the compounds. (Example: household cleanser contains sodium dichlore-s-triazinethrione dihydrate.) Students can find out the chemical formula, melting point, whether it is flammable, etc.

  Key Words: *chemical bonds, chemical bases, chemical acids, chemical compounds*

 Internet Resources

- *http://www.miamisci.org/af/sln/*—website about atoms and matter from the Miami Science Museum called The Atoms Family

- *http://www.webelements.com/*—website featuring an interactive periodic table

- *http://www.aps.org/*—the website of the American Physics Society; click the "Students & Educators" link for several educational resources

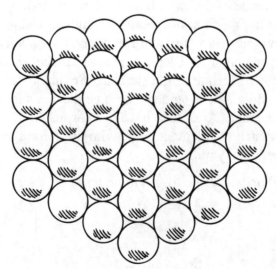

Matter

Student Introduction: Matter Word Web

Name: _____ **Date:** _____

Directions: Use this word web to help you brainstorm the characteristics of matter.

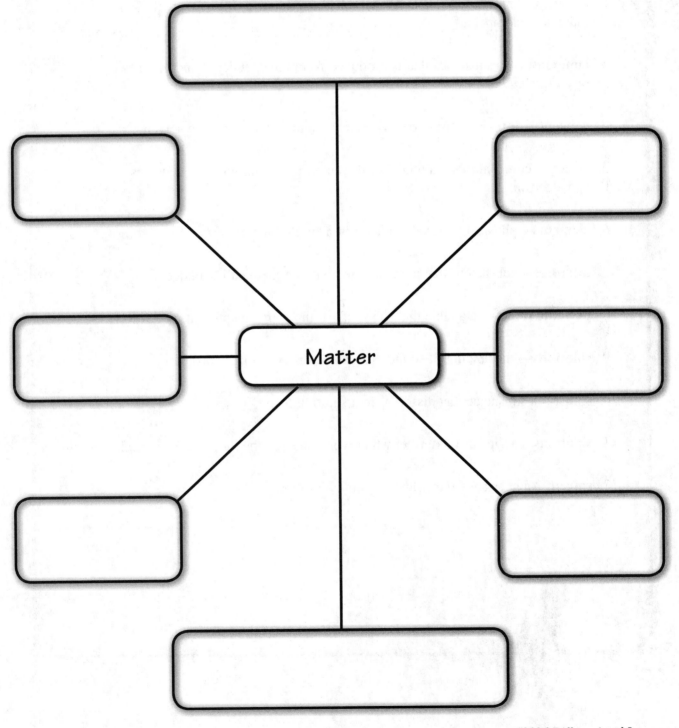

Matter

Vocabulary

1. **atomic number**—the amount of protons in a particular atom

2. **chemical formula**—a statement that tells how many atoms of each element make up a compound

3. **compound**—a substance that is produced from the chemical bonding of two or more elements

4. **concentration**—a measure of how much solute is dissolved in a solvent

5. **electron-cloud model**—a model of the atom, including protons, neutrons, and electrons

6. **elements**—physical material made up of a single type of atom

7. **mixtures**—substances that are combined but not chemically bonded

8. **periodic table**—data table that shows all of the elements present on Earth

9. **solubility**—the amount of solute that can be dissolved in a solvent

10. **solute**—a substance that dissolves in a solution

11. **solutions**—a type of mixture in which you can't see the individual materials

12. **solvent**—a substance into which a solute dissolves

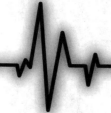

Matter

Brief #1: Atoms

Everything in the known universe is made up of tiny particles called atoms. You are made of atoms, and so is the planet Jupiter.

Atoms cannot be seen by the human eye without the help of special instruments, and this has made them very difficult to study. It has taken people over 2,000 years to understand atoms, and there are still many things that scientists are learning about the atom.

Vocabulary

1. electron-cloud model

Electron-Cloud Models

Scientists use models to help them study and learn about atoms. The type of model they use is called an electron-cloud model.

The electron-cloud model shows both areas of an atom. The nucleus of the atom is located in the center and is made of protons and neutrons. You may remember that a proton has a positive electrical charge and a neutron has no electrical charge at all.

Surrounding the nucleus in the model is the electron cloud. The electron cloud is the part of the atom that contains the electrons. Electrons have a negative electrical charge. There is also quite a bit of empty space between the electrons. The electrons orbit the nucleus of the atom.

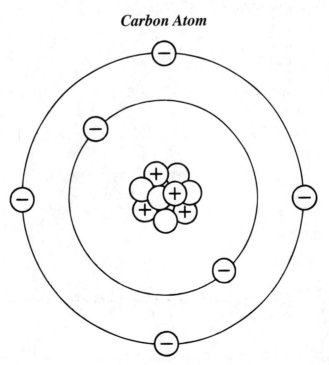

Carbon Atom

Matter

Brief #2: Elements

Elements are physical materials that are made up of a single type of atom. For example, iron is an element that is only made up of iron atoms. Carbon is an element that is only made up of carbon atoms.

So let's say, for example, that you could see the individual atoms in a piece of iron. What you would see are trillions of iron atoms, each one having a nucleus containing 26 protons and 26 neutrons, with 26 electrons orbiting that nucleus.

The number of protons in the nucleus of any type of atom is like its fingerprint. It is unique to that atom. If an atom has 6 protons it means that it makes the element called carbon. If an atom has 7 protons it makes the element called nitrogen.

There are only about 100 different types of natural elements present on Earth. Elements are considered pure substances because they are only made up of a single type of atom.

Vocabulary

1. elements
2. periodic table
3. atomic number

Types of Elements

Each of the elements has a different amount of protons and electrons. And different amounts of protons and electrons produce elements with different physical characteristics. For example, the element called mercury has 80 protons and 80 electrons. Mercury is a metallic liquid. The element of helium has 2 protons and 2 electrons. Helium is a nonmetallic gas. Elements can be metals, nonmetals, or metalloids.

Fast Fact

The human body contains the following elements:

✓ oxygen

✓ carbon

✓ hydrogen

✓ nitrogen

✓ calcium

✓ phosphorus

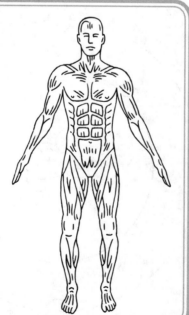

Metals are elements like copper, iron, and aluminum. They are usually hard, and strong. They are good conductors of electricity. Nonmetals are elements like selenium and helium. Nonmetals are not good conductors of electricity. Metalloids are elements that have characteristics of both metals and nonmetals.

Matter

Brief #2: Elements (cont.)

 The Periodic Table

The periodic table is a chart that lists all of the elements that are present on Earth.
This table also tells a lot of other information about the characteristics of the elements.

Atomic Number = Number of Protons = Number of Electrons

Atomic Number →
Chemical Symbol →
Chemical Name →

1
H
HYDROGEN

Non-Metals

Metals

Lanthanum Series

Actinide Series

Matter

Brief #2: Elements *(cont.)*

 ### The Periodic Table *(cont.)*

The periodic table is arranged in 7 rows and 18 columns. The elements in the columns are called families. They have certain things in common. The elements in the rows are called periods. They have very little in common.

Each element on the period table has an atomic number. **The atomic number tells how many protons are in the nucleus of that particular element.** The atomic number for sulfur is 16. That means that the sulfur atom has 16 protons in its nucleus. The elements are arranged from left to right in number order.

If you look carefully, about thee-quarters of the way across the period table, you will see a zig-zag line. All of the elements to the right of this line are non-metals. And all of the elements to the left of this line are metals. The elements that are along the zigzag line are the metalloids.

These are the metalloids:

✓ boron
✓ silicon
✓ germanium
✓ arsenic
✓ antimony
✓ tellurium
✓ polonium

atomic number
chemical symbol
element name

14
Si
SILICON

Silicon is a metalloid

Even though aluminum appears along this line, it is a metal.

 ### Lanthanum and Actinide Series

You have probably noticed that there are two rows that appear at the bottom of the periodic table that are separated from the rest. These are called the Lanthanum series and the Actinide series. The Lanthanum series goes from atomic number 57 to atomic number 71. This is really part of row six. It is the elements that come between barium and lutetium. The Actinide series is really part of row seven. It goes from atomic number 89 to atomic number 103. These two rows are pulled to the bottom of the periodic table only so that the periodic table can appear neatly over one page.

57 La LANTHANUM	58 Ce CERIUM	59 Pr PRASEODYMIUM	60 Nd NEODYMIUM	61 Pm PROMETHIUM	62 Sm SAMARIUM	63 Eu EUROPIUM	64 Gd Gadolinium	65 Tb TERBIUM	66 Dy DYSPROSIUM	67 Ho HOLMIUM	68 Er ERBIUM	69 Tm THULIUM	70 Yb YTTERBIUM	71 Lu LUTETIUM
89 Ac ACTINIUM	90 Th THORIUM	91 Pa PROTACTINIUM	92 U URANIUM	93 Np NEPTUNIUM	94 Pu PLUTONIUM	95 Am AMERICIUM	96 Cm CURIUM	97 Bk BERKELIUM	98 Cf CALIFORNIUM	99 Es EINSTEINIUM	100 Fm FERMIUM	101 Md Mendelevium	102 No NOBELIUM	103 Lr LAWRENCIUM

Matter

Brief #3: Compounds, Mixtures, and Solutions

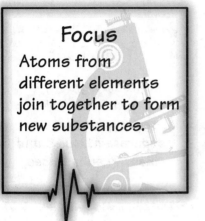

Focus
Atoms from different elements join together to form new substances.

Elements are pure substances that are formed from the same types of atoms. But the Earth is full of many other kinds of material that are combinations of more than one type of atom.

For example, when hydrogen and oxygen atoms come together in just the right quantities, water is produced. Water is not an element. Water is a compound.

Vocabulary
1. compound
2. chemical formula
3. mixtures
4. solutions
5. solute
6. solvent
7. concentration
8. solubility
9. pH scale

 Compounds

A compound is a substance that is produced from the bonding of two or more elements. In any chemical compound, every tiny particle of the substance has the exact ratio of elements as every other tiny particle in the substance.

Water is produced when two hydrogen atoms and one oxygen atom bond. That means that every drop of water, no matter where it is, has a ratio of 2 hydrogen atoms to 1 oxygen atom.

Every compound that is formed has a certain chemical formula. **A chemical formula tells how many atoms of each element make up the compound.**

Baking soda is a compound whose chemical formula is $NaHCO_3$. This means that baking soda is made of 1 sodium atom (Na), 1 hydrogen atom (H), 1 carbon atom (C), and 3 oxygen atoms (O_3).

Zinc sulfide is a compound whose formula is ZnS. This means that zinc sulfide is made from 1 zinc atom (Zn) and 1 sulfur atom (S).

In a chemical formula, the small numbers (for example, the "3" in "O_3") tell how many atoms are present for the element just before it. If no numbers appear, it means that only single atoms are present in the formula.

Matter

Brief #3: Compounds, Mixtures, and Solutions (cont.)

 ### Mixtures

Mixtures are substances that are not chemically bonded. When a substance is not chemically bonded it is easy to separate the different materials that are in the substance. For example, imagine scooping a teaspoon of baking soda in your hand.

Would you be able to separate the sodium from the hydrogen? It would be impossible to do this unless you used a special process. But mixtures are very different. Imagine if you scooped a teaspoon of trail mix into you hand. Would you be able to easily separate the raisins from the nuts? The answer is yes. That's because the materials that join in a mixture are not held together in a chemical bond.

> **Fast Fact**
>
> Chromatography is a collection of techniques that can separate mixtures and identify substances.

Mixtures may be made of elements or compounds. Mixtures may also be made of a combination of elements and compounds. Also, the different materials that form mixtures don't have a definite ratio. One handful of trail mix may have more nuts than another handful of trail mix.

Element	Compound	Mixture
□ □	□—○	□ ○
□ □	□—○	△ Σ
□ □	□—○	○ □
□ □	□—○	△ ♀
□ □	□—○	∽ ⊤

 ### Solutions

Solutions are mixtures in which you can't see the individual materials that make up the mixture. The materials in solutions are not chemically bonded; instead, one material dissolves into another, and this makes it difficult to see. Imagine if you put a teaspoon of sugar into a hot cup of tea. The sugar would dissolve into the tea so much that you would not be able to see it anymore. But if you took a sip of the tea, you sure would be able to taste it!

You can describe solutions by talking about the two parts that make up solutions. **The solute is the substance that dissolves. The sugar in that cup of tea is an example of the solute. The solvent is the substance into which the solute dissolves.** In this case, the tea would be the solvent.

Matter

Brief #3: Compounds, Mixtures, and Solutions *(cont.)*

 ### How Solutions Are Formed

So what really happens when you put a teaspoon of sugar in the hot tea? In other words, why does the sugar dissolve?

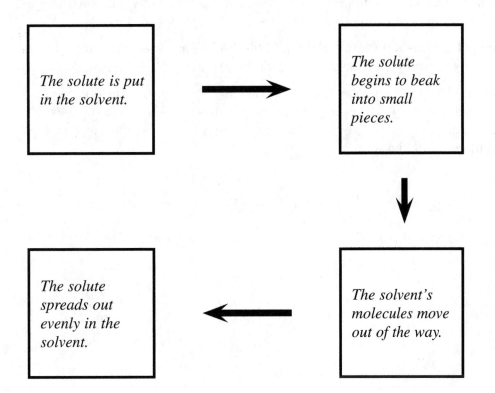

The solute is put in the solvent.

The solute begins to beak into small pieces.

The solvent's molecules move out of the way.

The solute spreads out evenly in the solvent.

 ### Concentration

Different solutions have different amounts of solute in them. **Concentration is a measurement of how much solute is dissolved in a solvent.** A cup of tea that contains three teaspoons of sugar has a higher concentration of solute than a cup of tea that contains one teaspoon of sugar.

Solubility is another property of solutions. **Solubility means how much of a solute can be dissolved in a solvent.** Imagine putting 20 teaspoonfuls of sugar in an 8-ounce cup of hot tea. Do you think all of the sugar would dissolve? Probably not. All solutions have a point at which there is too much solute to dissolve in the amount of solvent given.

Matter

Brief #3: Compounds, Mixtures, and Solutions *(cont.)*

 ### The pH Scale

Solutions can be studied and described by determining whether they are an acid or a base. An acid is a solution that has a strong reaction to metal, has a sour taste, and can sting or burn your skin. Lemon juice and other types of citrus juices are examples of acids. Bases are solutions that are slippery, taste bitter, and react strongly with oil and grease. Dishwashing liquid and other types of soaps are examples of bases.

The pH scale is a measure of acids and bases. This scale goes from 0 to 14. The lower the pH, the stronger the acid; the higher the pH, the stronger the base.

It is important to remember that both acids and bases can be harmful to you. Both can burn skin and irritate eyes. Never taste any acid or base unless you know what it is. Acids and bases can safely be tested with litmus paper. Acids turn blue litmus paper red. Bases turn red litmus paper blue.

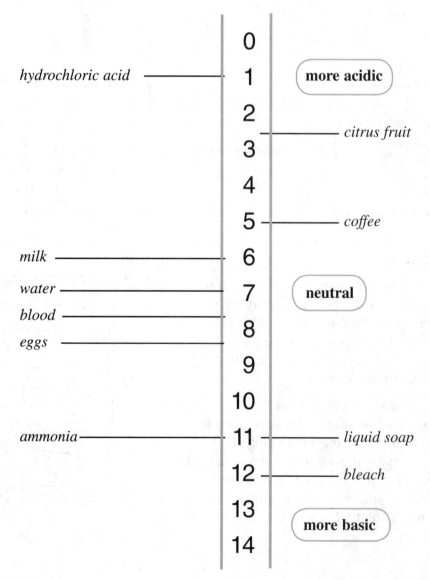

Matter

Multiple-Choice Assessment

Name: _____ **Date:** _____

Directions: Read each question carefully. Fill in the correct answer circle.

1. What is an atom?

   Ⓐ a molecule

   Ⓑ a proton

   Ⓒ a neutron

   Ⓓ smallest pieces of matter on Earth

   _____

2. What is an electron-cloud model?

   Ⓐ electrons located in clouds

   Ⓑ a model of the atom

   Ⓒ a model of a molecule

   Ⓓ a model of a nitrogen atom

   _____

3. What does an electron-cloud model show?

   Ⓐ protons, neutrons, and electrons

   Ⓑ electrons

   Ⓒ protons and electrons

   Ⓓ neutrons and electrons

   _____

4. What are elements made of?

   Ⓐ different types of atoms

   Ⓑ the same types of atoms

   Ⓒ different types of chemicals

   Ⓓ all of these

   _____

5. If an atom has 18 protons, how many electrons does it have?

   Ⓐ 8

   Ⓑ 32

   Ⓒ 18

   Ⓓ 2

Matter

Multiple-Choice Assessment *(cont.)*

6. How many different natural elements are there?

Ⓐ 110

Ⓑ 120

Ⓒ 100

Ⓓ 1,000

---

7. How can elements be classified?

Ⓐ as metals, liquids, and gases

Ⓑ as metals and non-metals

Ⓒ as alloys, compounds, and metalloids

Ⓓ as metals, non-metals, and metalloids

---

8. Which are the best conductors of electivity?

Ⓐ non-metals

Ⓑ mettaloids

Ⓒ metals

Ⓓ all conduct electricity well

---

9. What are the columns in the periodic table called?

Ⓐ periods

Ⓑ types

Ⓒ liquids

Ⓓ families

---

10. What is an atomic number?

Ⓐ the number of protons in an atom

Ⓑ the number of electrons in an atom

Ⓒ the number of neutrons on an atom

Ⓓ the combined number of neutrons and protons in an atom

Matter

Multiple-Choice Assessment *(cont.)*

11. Why are the Lanthanum and Actinide series set apart from the period table?

   Ⓐ They are manmade elements.

   Ⓑ The are not pure elements

   Ⓒ They are toxic elements.

   Ⓓ for convenience

---

12. How is a compound different from a mixture?

   Ⓐ One is a solution, the other is not.

   Ⓑ Compounds are chemically bonded, mixtures are not.

   Ⓒ Mixtures are chemically bonded, compounds are not.

   Ⓓ Compounds have more atoms than mixtures.

---

13. What are compounds made of?

   Ⓐ two or more different atoms

   Ⓑ one element

   Ⓒ one metal element

   Ⓓ one nonmetal element

---

14. What information does a chemical formula provide?

   Ⓐ the number of atoms in a compound

   Ⓑ the number of protons in a compound

   Ⓒ how many atoms of each element make up the compound

   Ⓓ none of these

---

15. What is a solution?

   Ⓐ a compound

   Ⓑ a solute

   Ⓒ a solvent

   Ⓓ a kind of mixture

Matter

Multiple-Choice Assessment *(cont.)*

16. What is a substance that dissolves called?

Ⓐ a solution

Ⓑ a solute

Ⓒ a solvent

Ⓓ a mixture

---

17. What is a solvent?

Ⓐ a substance that a solute dissolves into

Ⓑ a substance that a solution dissolves into

Ⓒ an acid solvent

Ⓓ a base solvent

---

18. What is concentration a measurement of?

Ⓐ acidity

Ⓑ density

Ⓒ atoms

Ⓓ how much solute can dissolve in a solvent

---

19. What does the pH scale measure?

Ⓐ bases

Ⓑ acids

Ⓒ toxins

Ⓓ acids and bases

---

20. If a solution is a 2 on the pH Scale, it is

Ⓐ a strong acid.

Ⓑ a strong base.

Ⓒ neutral.

Ⓓ none of these

Matter

Sentence-Completion Assessment

Name: _____ **Date:** _____

Directions: Read each statement. Fill in the word or words that best complete the sentence.

1. The smallest pieces of matter on Earth are called _____ .

2. A kind of model of the atoms is called an _____ .

3. Electrons have a _____ electrical charge.

4. If an atom has 18 protons then it has _____ electrons.

5. _____ are made of the same types of atoms.

6. There are about 100 natural _____ present on Earth.

7. Elements can be classified as metals, _____ , and _____ .

8. _____ are the best conductors of electricity.

9. The columns in the periodic table are called _____ .

10. The atomic number of an element tells how many _____ are in the atom.

Matter

Sentence-Completion Assessment *(cont.)*

11. The rows in the periodic table are called _____ .

12. Compounds are chemically _____ .

13. Compounds are made from different types of _____ .

14. A _____ tells how many atoms from each element made up a compound.

15. A solution is a kind of _____ .

16. A substance that dissolves is called a _____ .

17. A _____ is a substance that a solute dissolves into.

18. A measurement of how much solute can dissolve in a solvent is called _____ .

19. The pH scale measures _____ and _____ .

20. A solution that is a 2 on the pH scale is an _____

Matter

True-False Assessment

Name: _____ **Date:** _____

Directions: Read each statement carefully. If the statement is true, put a **T** on the line provided. If the statement is false, put an **F** on the line provided.

_____ **1.** Atoms are the smallest pieces of matter on Earth.

_____ **2.** An electron-cloud model is a model of an atom.

_____ **3.** An electron-cloud model shows only the electrons in atom.

_____ **4.** Elements are made of the same types of molecules.

_____ **5.** If an atom has 18 protons, it means it has 9 electrons.

_____ **6.** There are one thousand different kinds of elements.

_____ **7.** An element can be a metal, nonmetal, or metalloid.

_____ **8.** Metalloids are the best conductors of electricity.

_____ **9.** The columns in the periodic table are called families.

_____ **10.** An atomic number tells the number of protons in an atom.

GO

Matter

True-False Assessment

_____ **11.** The Lanthanum Series contains manmade elements.

_____ **12.** Compounds are chemically bonded.

_____ **13.** Compounds are made of the same types of atoms.

_____ **14.** A chemical formula tells how many neutrons are in a compound.

_____ **15.** A solution is a kind of mixture.

_____ **16.** A solute dissolves in a solvent.

_____ **17.** A solvent is always an acid.

_____ **18.** A concentration measures how much solute can dissolve in a solvent.

_____ **19.** The pH scale measures acids and bases.

_____ **20.** If a solution is a 2 on the pH scale, it means that it is a strong base.

Matter

Matching Assessment

Name: _____   Date: _____

Directions: Read the items in both lists below and on page 132 carefully. Choose an item from List B that best matches an item from List A. Write the corresponding letter from List B on the line. You will have some left over.

List A	List B
_____ 1. atom	**A.** Actinide series
_____ 2. electron-cloud model	**B.** number of protons
_____ 3. elements	**C.** dissolves
_____ 4. helium	**D.** lemon juice
_____ 5. types of elements	**E.** a nonmetallic gas
_____ 6. good electricity conductors	**F.** litmus paper
_____ 7. periodic table columns	**G.** compound fingerprint
_____ 8. periodic table rows	**H.** families
_____ 9. atomic number	**I.** smallest pieces of matter
_____ 10. compound	**J.** easily separated
_____ 11. chemical formula	**K.** dissolver
_____ 12. solution	**L.** metals

GO

Matter

Matching Assessment *(cont.)*

List A	List B
_____ **13.** solute	**M.** Lanthanum series
_____ **14.** solvent	**N.** metals, nonmetals, metalloids
_____ **15.** concentration	**O.** pure substances
_____ **16.** pH scale	**P.** chemical bonding
_____ **17.** solubility	**Q.** liquid soap
_____ **18.** mixtures	**R.** acids and bases
_____ **19.** acid example	**S.** type of mixture
_____ **20.** base example	**T.** how much solute can dissolve
	U. atom model
	V. type of measure
	W. periods

Matter

Graphic Assessment

Name: _____ **Date:** _____

Directions: In the box below, draw an electron-cloud model for the element shown here. Label all of the parts.

```
┌─────────────────┐
│                 │
│       16        │
│                 │
│        S        │
│                 │
│     Sulfur      │
│                 │
└─────────────────┘
```

Matter

Short-Response Assessment

Name: _____ **Date:** _____

Directions: Read each question carefully. Write a short response of a few sentences to each question.

1. Describe the periodic table in as much detail as possible.

_____

_____

_____

_____

_____

2. Describe a compound. Provide an example including a chemical formula. Tell what the chemical formula means.

_____

_____

_____

_____

_____

3. Explain the difference between a mixture and a solution. Provide examples.

_____

_____

_____

_____

4. Describe atoms and their elements. What makes one atom or element different than another? What are atoms made of? What is the structure of an atom?

_____

_____

_____

_____

Machines

Teacher Materials

 ### Teacher Preparation

Before you begin this unit, photocopy and distribute the following to students:

- Student Introduction (pages 138–139)
- Unit Vocabulary (page 140)
- Student Briefs (pages 141–144)
- Appropriate Assessments (pages 145–156)

 ### Key Unit Concepts

- *Work* is a pushing or pulling force that moves an object.
- The formula to calculate work is "force multiplied by distance."
- Work is measured in units called *joules.*
- *Machines* are devices that help people do work.
- The *wedge, screw, inclined plane, pulley, wheel and axle,* and *lever* are the six simple machines that are made of one or two parts.
- Simple machines decrease the amount of force a person has to exert to move an object.
- A *compound machine* is often made of many simple machines.
- The *fulcrum, effort force,* and the *load* are in different locations in first-class, second-class, and third-class levers.

 ### Discussion Topics

- Brainstorm a list of simple tool machines that you see used every day.
- List some of the simple machines that are present in more compound machines that you see every day.

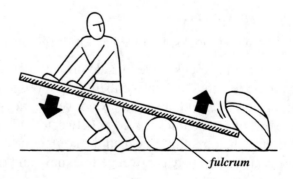

fulcrum

See "Generic Strategies and Activities" on pages 8 and 9 for additional strategies useful to presenting this unit.

Machines

Activities

 Brief #1: Work

- **Problem Solving:** Have students complete the "Work Problem-Solving" activity sheet on page 138.

- **Design a Compound Machine:** Have students invent a compound machine that is made up of at least three simpler machines. Ask them to draw their compound machine on a large piece of poster board. Make sure that they label all of the parts and explain the task the machine performs.

  Key Words: *compound machines*

 Brief #2: Simple Machines

- **List Simple Machines:** Have students take a walk around the school building and keep track of all the simple machines that they see. Upon returning to the classroom, have studens use butcher paper to create a mural of all of the simple machines that they spotted.

- **Disassemble a Toy:** Ask students to bring in an old toy or appliance to class. Using screwdrivers, pliers, and other tools, have them take apart the item and list all of the parts that are present.

- **Perform an Experiment:**

  Supplies: ruler, pencil, 50 pennies

  Procedure: Make a lever by placing the pencil (the fulcrum) beneath the ruler (the lever) at the 4-inch mark. Place 10 pennies on the 1-inch mark at one end of the ruler. This is the load. Ask students to speculate about how many pennies will be needed to lift the load. Have students add pennies to the opposite end of the ruler to test their theory. Students should record their results. Ask students to repeat the experiment several times by moving the fulcrum to different locations on the lever to see how that impacts how many pennies are needed to lift the load.

- **Perform an Experiment:**

  Supplies: two wood blocks, two wedges of different thicknesses, a ruler

  Procedure: Place the blocks side by side on your desk. Measure how long the blocks are. Record the length. Now, place the thinner wedge between the blocks. Measure the blocks again. Record the length. Remove the wedge and push the blocks back together. Now, place the thicker wedge between the blocks. Record the length. Have students discuss the direction in which the wedge moved the blocks. Have them discuss the relationship between wedge thickness and distance between objects.

Machines

Activities *(cont.)*

 Brief #2: Simple Machines *(cont.)*

- **Perform an Experiment:**

    Supplies: textbooks, beans or rice in a small plastic baggie tied tightly closed, rubber band, ruler

    Procedure: Stack some textbooks on top of each other. Prop another textbook against them to create an inclined plane. Tie a rubber band around the top of the plastic baggie full of beans or rice. Lift the baggie straight up from the bottom of the pile of textbooks to the top. Measure the length of the rubber band to see how much it has stretched. Record the length. Next, drag the baggie up the inclined plane that was created out of the textbooks. When it is at the very top, measure the length of the rubber band. Record the results. Discuss what conclusions can be drawn about the different lengths of the rubber bands.

- **Perform an Experiment:**

    Supplies: block of wood, hammer, nail, screw

    Procedure: Speculate about which will be easier to hammer into the wood, the screws or the nails. First, try to hammer a screw into the wood. Next, try to hammer a nail. Draw conclusions about why the nail could be hammered and the screw not. (The screw is an inclined plane. The nail is really a wedge and can split the wood apart.)

    Key Words: *simple machines, levers, screws, wedges, inclined planes*

 Internet Resources

- *http://sunshine.chpc.utah.edu/javalabs/java12/machine/index.htm* — interactive website about simple machines; from University of Utah students

- *http://www.mos.org/sln/Leonardo/InventorsWorkshop.html* — the Inventor's Workshop from the Museum of Science; includes classroom activities and interactive games

- -

Answer Key for "Work Problem-Solving" worksheet (page 138):

1.	235.2	**4.**	12	**7.**	323	**10.**	2,691
2.	425	**5.**	279	**8.**	3,799	**11.**	68
3.	242	**6.**	9	**9.**	42	**12.**	6

Machines

Student Introduction: Work Problem-Solving

Name: _____ **Date:** _____

Directions: Find the solutions to the problems below. Show your work.

1. 7.35 (N) x 32 (m) = _____ (J)	**7.** 2,907 (J) = _____ (N) x 9 (m)
2. 17 (m) x 25 (N) = _____ (J)	**8.** 131 (km) x 29 (N) = _____ (J)
3. 18,150 (J) = 75 (N) x _____ (km)	**9.** 378 (J) = _____ (m) x 9 (N)
4. 17 (m) x _____ (N) = 204 (J)	**10.** 207 (N) x 13 (m) = _____ (J)
5. 93 (N) x 3 (m) = _____ (J)	**11.** 7 (N) = _____ (J) x 476 (m)
6. 63 (N) x _____ (m) = 567 (J)	**12.** 35 (m) x _____ (N) = 210 (J)

STOP

138

Machines

Student Introduction: Machines Word Web

Name: _____ **Date:** _____

Directions: Use this word web to help you brainstorm the characteristics of machines.

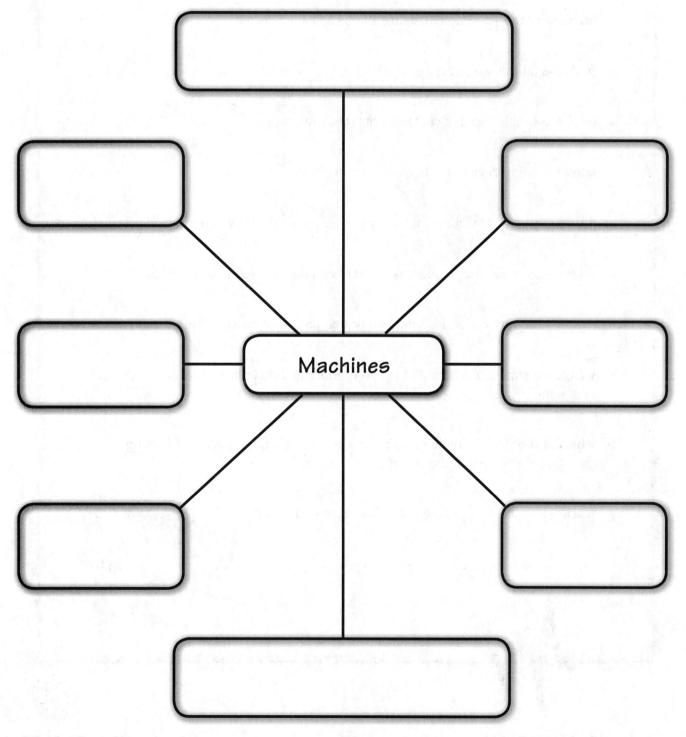

Machines

Vocabulary

1. **compound machine**—a machine that is made up of two or more simple machines

2. **inclined plane**—a simple machine that is a slanted surface

3. **joule**—a unit measurement of work

4. **lever**—a simple, rigid device that contains a fulcrum

5. **machine**—any device that helps people do work

6. **pulley**—a simple machine that is made of a grooved wheel and a rope or cable

7. **screw**—a simple machine that is an inclined plane curved in a spiral shape

8. **simple machine**—a device with one or two parts that moves a single load

9. **wedge**—a simple machine that is two or more inclined planes that come together in a point

10. **wheel and axle**—a simple machine that is a wheel and a shaft or rod that goes through (or is joined to the center of) the wheel

11. **work**—a pushing or pulling force that moves an object

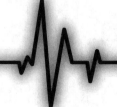

Machines

Brief #1: Work

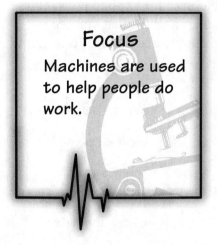

Right at this moment you may think that you are working hard to understand what you are reading. But a scientist would tell you that thinking doesn't count as work. In fact, that same scientist would probably say that the only work that you are doing right at this moment is turning the page!

This is because scientists have a very special way of defining what counts as work. **In science, "work" is using a pushing or pulling force to move an object.**

Vocabulary

1. work
2. joule
3. machine
4. simple machine
5. compound machine

You can use a formula to calculate how much work has been done. Here is the formula that you use:

> **work = force x distance**

Work is measured in units called joules. The abbreviation for joule is J.

> **1 joule (J) = 1 Newton (N) x 1 meter (m)**

 ### Machines

You may not think of scissors or a bottle opener as machines, but they are!

A machine is any kind of device that helps people to do work. Machines help people push and pull and move heavy loads. There are simple machines and compound machines.

A simple machine is a device with one or two parts that work to move a single load. A compound machine is made up of one or more simple machines that work together to push and/or pull.

Simple machines can help people to do work because they decrease the amount of force needed to move a load.

Imagine if you needed to move a load of bricks from the ground to the second floor of a building. Which do you think would require less force—carrying the brick up two flights of stairs or pulling the brick up a ramp?

If you guessed using a ramp, you are correct. That's because the force needed is applied over a greater distance. Using a ramp to move a load is a kind of trade-off. Less force is needed, but the bricks have to be moved farther than if they were lifted vertically.

Machines

Brief #2: Simple Machines

There are six different kinds of simple machines. Simple machines help people to do work. Any compound machine that you see is made up of several different types of simple machines. Here are the six types of simple machines:

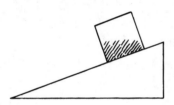

✓ inclined plane

✓ wedge

✓ screw

✓ wheel and axle

✓ lever

✓ pulley

Vocabulary

1. inclined plane
2. wedge
3. screw
4. wheel and axle
5. lever
6. pulley

 ### Inclined Plane

An inclined plane is a ramp or any type of slanted surface. Inclined planes are used to move heavy loads or people vertically. Inclined planes have no moving parts. Roller coasters contain several inclined planes.

 ### Wedge

A wedge is two or more inclined planes that come together in a point. Wedges can be used to split or "wedge" materials apart. Wedges can also be used to stop something from moving. A doorstop is an example of a wedge.

 ### Screw

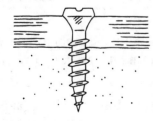

A screw is another simple machine that has no moving parts. **A screw is an inclined plane that is curved in a spiral.** Screws move things up and down. The raised parts on the screw are called threads. Most light bulbs have a screw on the end that allows them to be lowered down into or raised up out of a socket. The threads on the screw help to hold the bulb in place.

Machines

Brief #2: Simple Machines *(cont.)*

 Wheel and Axle

A wheel and axle is a simple machine that is made up of a wheel and a shaft or rod that goes through the center of the wheel or is joined to the center of a wheel.

The diameter of the wheel part of this machine is always much larger than the diameter of the axle. This allows a person to turn a larger wheel through a bigger space by turning a smaller wheel through a smaller space.

 Lever

A lever is a rigid device that has a fulcrum, which is a kind of pivot. A playground seesaw is a type of lever. There are three different kinds of levers. The thing that makes them different from one another is the location of the effort force, the fulcrum, and the load.

✓ In a first-class lever, the effort force and the load are at opposite ends and the fulcrum is in the middle. A crow bar and the hand brakes on a bicycle are examples of first-class levers.

✓ In a second-class lever, the effort force and the fulcrum are at opposite ends and the load is in the middle. A diving board and a nutcracker are examples of second-class levers.

✓ In a third-class lever, the fulcrum and the load are at opposite ends and the force is applied in the middle. A stapler and tweezers are examples of third-class levers.

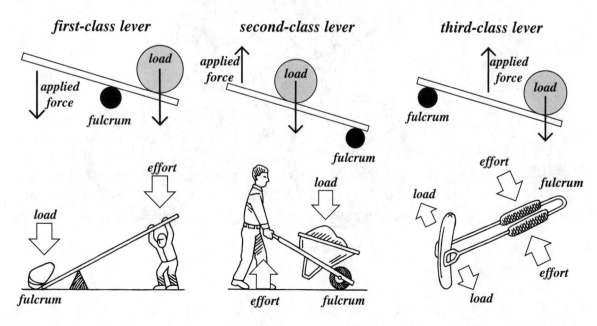

Machines

Brief #2: Simple Machines *(cont.)*

 ### Pulley

A pulley is a simple machine that helps to lift and lower heavy loads. **A pulley is made of a rope or cable that is placed over a grooved wheel.** The load is attached to one end of the pulley, and the force is applied to the other. An escalator uses a belt and pulley systems to move people vertically.

Compound Machines

A compound machine is a devise that is made of several simple machines. Cars, trains, buses, and boats are all examples of compound machines.

lever

screw

pulley

wheel and axle

Machines

Multiple-Choice Assessment

Name: _____   **Date:** _____

Directions: Read each question carefully. Fill in the correct answer circle.

1. According to the definition given in this unit, which of the following activities is considered "work"?

   Ⓐ doing mental math

   Ⓑ dreaming

   Ⓒ playing a video game

   Ⓓ none of these

2. What is the formula to calculate work?

   Ⓐ joule x distance – work

   Ⓑ work = force x distance

   Ⓒ Newton x joule = work

   Ⓓ joule x 1 meter = work

3. What is a joule?

   Ⓐ a measurement of force

   Ⓑ a measurement of distance

   Ⓒ a measurement of gravity

   Ⓓ a measurement of work

4. What is a machine?

   Ⓐ motorized devices only

   Ⓑ a device with only two parts

   Ⓒ any device that helps people do work

   Ⓓ all of these

5. What is a simple machine?

   Ⓐ a device with one or two parts that moves a single load

   Ⓑ a device with three or more parts that moves a single load

   Ⓒ a machine made of one or more simple machines that push or pull

   Ⓓ any machine that pushes or pulls

Machines

Multiple-Choice Assessment *(cont.)*

6. How do simple machines help people do work?

Ⓐ They increase the force needed to move a load.

Ⓑ They increase the load needed to move a load.

Ⓒ They decrease the force of gravity needed to move a load.

Ⓓ They decrease the amount of force needed to move a load.

---

7. How many types of simple machines are there?

Ⓐ 10

Ⓑ 2

Ⓒ 6

Ⓓ 100

---

8. Which of the following is not a simple machine?

Ⓐ lever

Ⓑ screw

Ⓒ inclined plane

Ⓓ bike

---

9. In order for work to be done what has to happen?

Ⓐ force must be applied on an object

Ⓑ an object must move

Ⓒ an object must have mass

Ⓓ none of these

---

10. What is an inclined plane?

Ⓐ a slanted surface that is curved around a spiral

Ⓑ a wheel with a shaft

Ⓒ a slanted surface

Ⓓ a grooved wheel and a cable

Machines

Multiple-Choice Assessment *(cont.)*

11. Which of the following machines has raised parts called threads?

   Ⓐ a screw

   Ⓑ a wheel and axle

   Ⓒ a lever

   Ⓓ a winch

12. In a wheel and axle,

   Ⓐ the diameter of the wheel is greater than the diameter of the axle.

   Ⓑ the diameter of the axle is greater than the diameter of the wheel.

   Ⓒ the diameter of the wheel and the diameter of the axle are equal.

   Ⓓ the circumference of the wheel is half the circumference of the axle.

13. Which of the following is most closely related to an inclined plane?

   Ⓐ a lever

   Ⓑ a pulley

   Ⓒ a wedge

   Ⓓ a second-class lever

14. What simple machines have no moving parts?

   Ⓐ wheel and axle

   Ⓑ screw

   Ⓒ inclined plane

   Ⓓ both B and C

15. What is a fulcrum?

   Ⓐ a lever

   Ⓑ a screw

   Ⓒ a pivot

   Ⓓ a grooved wheel

Machines

Multiple-Choice Assessment *(cont.)*

16. How many different types of levers are there?

Ⓐ 2

Ⓑ 3

Ⓒ 9

Ⓓ 1

---

17. In what way do levers differ from one another?

Ⓐ the location of the fulcrum

Ⓑ the location of the load

Ⓒ the location of the effort force

Ⓓ all of these

---

18. Where is the fulcrum located in a first-class lever?

Ⓐ at the opposite end of the effort force

Ⓑ at the opposite end of the load

Ⓒ in the middle of the effort force and the load

Ⓓ under the grooved wheel

---

19. A simple machine that has the effort force and the fulcrum at opposite ends is

Ⓐ a first-class lever.

Ⓑ a third-class lever.

Ⓒ a second-class lever.

Ⓓ a wedge lever.

---

20. Which is an example of a third-class lever?

Ⓐ a crow bar

Ⓑ a diving board

Ⓒ a stapler

Ⓓ a nutcracker

Machines

Sentence-Completion Assessment

Name: _____   **Date:** _____

Directions: Read each statement. Fill in the word or words that best complete the sentence.

1. Work is done when a _____ or _____ force moves an object.

2. Work = _____ x _____ .

3. Work is measured in _____ .

4. A device that helps people to do work is called a _____ .

5. A simple machine moves a _____ load.

6. Simple machines _____ the amount of force needed to move a load.

7. There are _____ types of simple machines.

8. A lever, _____, wheel and axle, _____,
   _____, and a _____

   are all simple machines.

9. An inclined plane is a _____ surface.

10. A simple machine with raised threads is called a _____ .

(GO)

Machines

Sentence-Completion Assessment *(cont.)*

11. In a wheel and axle, the diameter of the _____

is greater than the diameter of the _____ .

12. A _____ is made of two or more inclined planes.

13. A _____ is a simple machine with no moving parts.

14. A pivot is also called a _____ .

15. There are _____ different types of levers.

16. Different types of levers have the effort force, the _____ and the

_____ in different locations.

17. In a _____ lever, the fulcrum is in the middle, between the force and the load.

18. In a _____ lever, the force and the fulcrum are at opposite ends.

19. In a _____ lever, the fulcrum and the load are at opposite ends.

20. A stapler is an example of a _____ lever.

Machines

True-False Assessment

Name: _____ **Date:** _____

Directions: Read each statement carefully. If the statement is true, put a **T** on the line provided. If the statement is false, put an **F** on the line provided.

_____ **1.** An object must move for work to be done.

_____ **2.** Work = newton x distance.

_____ **3.** A joule is a measurement of force.

_____ **4.** A machine is any device that helps people do work.

_____ **5.** A simple machine moves a single load.

_____ **6.** Simple machines increase the amount of force needed to move a load.

_____ **7.** There are six different types of simple machines.

_____ **8.** A lever is not a simple machine.

_____ **9.** An inclined plane is a slanted surface.

_____ **10.** A screw has raised threads.

Machines

True-False Assessment *(cont.)*

_____ **11.** The diameter of the axle is always greater than the diameter of the wheel.

_____ **12.** A wedge is similar to a pulley.

_____ **13.** A wheel and axle has no moving parts.

_____ **14.** A fulcrum is a pivot.

_____ **15.** There are five different types of levers.

_____ **16.** Levers differ in the location of the fulcrum, effort force, and load.

_____ **17.** A first-class lever has the fulcrum and load at opposite ends.

_____ **18.** A second-class lever has the force and the fulcrum at opposite ends.

_____ **19.** A third-class lever has the fulcrum in the middle of the force and the load.

_____ **20.** A stapler is an example of a third-class lever.

Machines

Matching Assessment

Name: _____   **Date:** _____

Directions: Read the items in both lists below and on page 154 carefully. Choose an item from List B that best matches an item from List A. Write the corresponding letter from List B on the line. You will have some left over.

List A	List B
_____ 1. work	**A.** force applied in the middle
_____ 2. work formula	**B.** third-class lever
_____ 3. joule	**C.** decrease force
_____ 4. definition of "machine"	**D.** newtons
_____ 5. simple machine	**E.** bicycle
_____ 6. purpose of simple machines	**F.** pushing or pulling force
_____ 7. number of simple machines	**G.** six
_____ 8. slanted surface	**H.** pivot
_____ 9. simple machine with raised threads	**I.** measure of work
_____ 10. simple machine with grooved wheel	**J.** second-class lever
_____ 11. inclined plane relative	**K.** one or two parts
_____ 12. fulcrum	**L.** three

GO

Machines

Matching Assessment *(cont.)*

List A	List B
_____ **13.** nutcracker	**M.** fulcrum located in middle
_____ **14.** number of lever types	**N.** meter
_____ **15.** first-class lever	**O.** force x distance
_____ **16.** second-class lever	**P.** wedge
_____ **17.** third-class lever	**Q.** pulley
_____ **18.** stapler	**R.** screw
_____ **19.** compound machine	**S.** device that helps do work
	T. inclined plane
	U. load is located in middle

STOP

Machines

Graphic Assessment

Name: _____ **Date:** _____

Directions: Draw three illustrations that depict the three different types of levers. Label the parts of the levers.

first-class lever

second-class lever

third-class lever

Machines

Short-Response Assessment

Name: _____ **Date:** _____

Directions: Read each question carefully. Write a short response of a few sentences to each question.

1. Name three simple machines. Select one and describe how it might be used to do work.

   _____

   _____

   _____

   _____

   _____

2. Name the three types of levers. Explain how each works.

   _____

   _____

   _____

   _____

   _____

3. Make a list of at least six simple machines that you see in your classroom.

   _____

   _____

   _____

   _____

   _____

4. If you could only take one simple machine on a camping trip, which one would it be? Explain your answer.

   _____

   _____

   _____

   _____

   _____

Force and Motion

Teacher Materials

 Teacher Preparation

Before you begin this unit, photocopy and distribute the following to students:

- Student Introduction (page 160)
- Unit Vocabulary (page 161)
- Student Briefs (pages 162–172)
- Appropriate Assessments (pages 173–186)

 Key Unit Concepts

- *Gravity, electricity, magnetism,* and *friction* are types of forces.
- *Contact* and *action-at-a-distance* describe different forces.
- Usually more than one force acts on an object.
- *Net forces* are all of the forces that act on an object.
- Rolling, sliding, and static friction slow objects down.
- *Friction* creates heat.
- *Lubricants* help to reduce friction.
- *Coefficients* describe friction.
- Tides are affected by the gravitational force.
- A frame of reference is needed to describe motion.
- *Circular, uniform,* and *vibratory* are types of motion.
- *Speed, velocity,* and *acceleration* are measures of motion.
- Isaac Newton described the connection between force and motion.
- There are three laws of motion.

 Discussion Topics

- Brainstorm a list of all of the forces that are at work in your classroom right at this very moment.
- Discuss the nature of motion. What is the fastest/slowest you have ever gone? Describe the motion that is a part of your everyday life.

See "Generic Strategies and Activities" on pages 8 and 9 for additional strategies useful to presenting this unit.

Force and Motion

Activities

 Brief #1: Forces

- **Make an Informational Poster:** Using poster board and paint or markers, make a poster that illustrates both contact forces and action-at-a-distance forces.

- **Write a Research Brief:** Research the Olympic event called the decathlon. Write a two-page research brief that explains the events and describes the forces and motions involved in each. You many include illustrations or other visual elements in your brief.

  Key Words: *contact forces, action-at-a-distance forces, decathlon*

 Brief #2: Friction

- **Perform an Experiment:**

  Supplies: two glass bowls, water, a tennis ball, a smooth rubber ball

  Procedure: Fill the glass bowls halfway with water. Put one ball in each bowl. Spin each ball. Observe what happens. (The smooth ball will spin more quickly and easily because there is less friction due to the smooth surface.)

- **Perform an Experiment:**

  Supplies: piece of wooden board about two feet long; meter- or yardstick; tape; stopwatch; sandpaper (of the same length as the wooden board); an assortment of objects (plastic building toys, toy cars, pens, etc.)

  Procedure: Make an incline with the wooden board. Place the meter- or yardstick next to the incline. Take each object and slide it down the surface. Measure how far the objects slides and how long it takes. Record your results. Next, cover the wooden board with the sandpaper and repeat the same experiment. Note the differences in the object's ability to slide down a rough surface versus a smooth surface.

  Key Words: *friction*

 Brief #3: Gravity

- **Perform an Experiment:**

  Supplies: stopwatch, an assortment of objects of different weights and sizes (e.g., different-sized balls, paper clips, pens, rocks), scale

  Procedure: Weigh and record the weight of each object. Drop each object from a specific height. Record how long it takes each object to hit the ground. (Each object, regardless of mass, should hit the ground at the same time.) After students have completed this experiment, have them research Galileo and his gravity experiments. Ask them to write a short research brief that describes their experiments and how their findings were consistent with Galileo's.

Force and Motion

Activities *(cont.)*

 Brief #4: Motion

- **Go on a Motion Scavenger Hunt:** Take a walk in your school or community and write down as many examples as you can see of circular, uniform, and vibratory motion.

   Key Words: *circular motion, uniform motion, vibratory motion*

 Brief #5: Newton's Laws of Motion

- **Perform an Experiment:**

   Supplies: a glass of water, a pie pan, a cardboard tube (from toilet paper), a raw egg

   Procedure: Place the pie pan on top of the glass of water. Place the cardboard tube in the middle of the pie pan right over the water. Place the egg on the top of the tube. Whack the side of the pie pan with the hand you write with. Give it a good whack. The pie plate will fly sideways, the cardboard tube will topple, and the egg will fall directly into the water. This experiment demonstrates Newton's first law of motion: that an object at rest will want to remain at rest. This is why the egg doesn't move. It stays put and the force of gravity pulls it down into the glass of water. (*Note:* If you wish to eliminate the possibility of breaking eggs in the classroom, a small, egg-sized ball could be used instead.)

- **Create Laws of Motion:** Pretend you are an explorer that is studying life on a planet in another galaxy. Force and motion are different on this distant planet. Explain the laws of motion that exist on this planet.

   Key Words: *law of inertia, Newton's laws of motion*

 Internet Resources

- *http://www.physicsclassroom.com/* — contains detailed explanations to all kinds of physics questions

- *http://www.aip.org/history/* — website of the American Institute of Physics

- *http://www.fearofphysics.com/* — the Fear of Physics website, which contains entertaining information and demonstrations for students

Force and Motion

Student Introduction: Force and Motion Word Web

Name: _____   **Date:** _____

Directions: Use this word web to help you brainstorm characteristics of force and motion.

Force and Motion

Force and Motion

Vocabulary

1. **acceleration**—a measurement of how velocity changes over time

2. **circular motion**—motion that travels around a central point

3. **force**—a push or a pull

4. **friction**—a force that is the result of objects pressing tightly against each other

5. **inertia**—the tendency of an object to resist a change in its motion

6. **momentum**—the motion of mass

7. **net forces**—all of the different forces acting on an object

8. **rolling friction**—the result of an object being rolled across a surface

9. **sliding friction**—the result of an object being slid across a surface

10. **speed**—the measure of how fast an object moves over a given amount of time

11. **static friction**—the result of an object that is at rest and just begins to move

12. **uniform motion**—motion that travels in a straight line

13. **velocity**—the measurement of the speed and direction of an object

14. **vibratory motion**—the rapid back-and-forth motion of objects

Force and Motion

Brief #1: Forces

Focus

Forces act on all objects in the universe.

The universe in which we live is full of all different kinds of forces. **A force is a push or a pull.** There is the force of gravity. Gravity is a pulling force. And there is the force of magnetism, which can push or pull. Some forces are big, like the force that keeps the Earth in orbit around the sun. Some forces can be much smaller, like the force that keeps electrons orbiting the nucleus of an atom.

Some forces act only if the objects involved are touching each other. These are called contact forces. If you hit a tennis ball with a racket, the racket and the ball have come into contact with one another.

Vocabulary

1. force

2. net forces

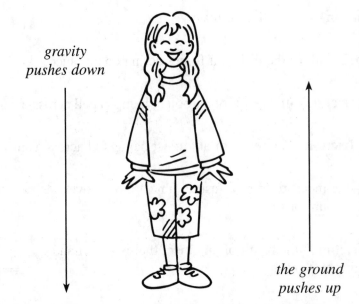

gravity pushes down

the ground pushes up

But there are other forces that can act on objects without having to be in contact with them. These are called action-at-a-distance forces. For example, if you put two magnets close together, you will be able to feel the push or pull without the magnets having to touch. Force is always the result of the interactions of objects with one another, whether they are touching or not.

Forces have size and direction. The size of a force is measured in newtons. "N" is the abbreviation for "newton." One newton is equal to the amount of force it would take to move an object with a mass of one kilogram a distance of one meter every second.

A spring scale can be used to measure forces. An object is attached to one end of the spring scale. The spring stretches to show how much force is pulling down on the object.

Force and Motion

Brief #1: Forces *(cont.)*

 ### Net Forces

It is rare for there to be only one type of force acting on any object. Most of the time, many forces are acting on an object at a given time. **All of the different forces acting on an object are called net forces.**

In the illustration above, you can see all of the forces that are acting on the boat: the force of gravity is pushing down, the force of the water is pushing up, and the wind is blowing from east to west and from west to east.

If the boat moves west, it is because wind is blowing from the east. If the boat doesn't move at all, it means that there is no wind blowing from either direction or that the same amount of wind is blowing from each direction. When forces are unbalanced, an object at rest will move. But when forces are balanced, the motion of the object will not change.

If you take a look again at the picture above, you will see that there is a 12 N force pushing to the west and an 8 N force pushing to the east.

To figure out the net forces on the sailboat, you subtract the forces. The result is that there is 4 N force pushing to the west. The net force is 4 N to the west.

The net forces on any object can act to change the direction of an object or can slow an object down.

Force and Motion

Brief #2: Friction

Focus

Friction is a contact force that resists movement.

If you have ever rollerskated, ridden a bike, or rolled a bowling ball down an alley, you have seen friction in action. **Friction is a force that is the result of objects pressing tightly against each other. The force of friction slows things down.**

There are three different types of friction:

✓ rolling

✓ sliding

✓ static

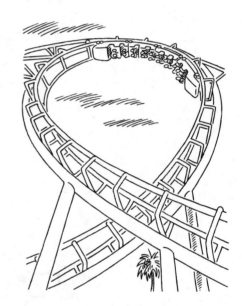

Rolling friction is the result of an object being rolled across a surface. The wheels of a roller coaster rolling along a steel track are an example of rolling friction.

Sliding friction is the result of an object being slid across a surface. If you push your science textbook across the floor of the room, you will create sliding friction.

Static friction is the result of an object that is at rest and just begins to move. If there is a box full of bricks in the middle of the school hallway and you begin to push it forward, static friction will result.

How much friction is present depends on two things:

✓ the material each object and surface is made of

✓ how tightly the object and the surface pressed together

Let's go back to our example of sliding friction. Your textbook may slide quite easily across the floor of your classroom, especially if the surface of the book and the floor are smooth. But what might happen if you put a brick on top of your book and then tried to slide it? If you guessed that the book would not slide as easily, you are correct. The more tightly together the objects are pressed, the greater the friction will be. Rougher surfaces also create greater friction.

Vocabulary

1. friction
2. rolling friction
3. sliding friction
4. static friction

Force and Motion

Brief #2: Friction *(cont.)*

 ### Friction in Everyday Life

Friction may sound like not such a great thing because it can slow things down or make them stop. But think for a minute what would happen in our everyday lives if friction were not a part of it! Imagine what would happen to the players in a basketball game if there was no friction between their feet and the court. The truth is that the shoes these players wear are specially designed with friction in mind.

A surface that is made of rubber has more friction because rubber easily bends. This friction created by contact between the rubber soles and the wooden court helps the basketball players stop and start more easily.

Of course, the opposite would be true with the sport of ice hockey. Ice skates are designed to reduce friction upon contact with the ice. As the blade of the skate moves across the ice, the friction created causes it to heat up. This little bit of heat melts the ice directly beneath the skate, and the water acts as a lubricant. This reduces friction and allows the skates to slide easier. The water refreezes as soon as the blade of the skate is no longer in contact with it.

You know if you rub your palms together that they will heat up a little bit. This is the result of friction. Sometimes the friction between two objects can cause so much heat that a fire can start. After any kind of motorized machine has been running for a while, it will give off a certain amount of heat. The heat is a result of all of the parts of the machine rubbing together and creating friction.

For this reason, many mechanized devices have to use lubricants to reduce friction. Cars, buses, and trucks use oil. Grease is used to lubricate the gears in other types of machines. There is a whole branch of science called *tribology* that studies the connection between friction and lubricant.

Fast Fact

The coefficient of friction means how easily one object moves over another object.

high coefficient = higher friction

low coefficient = lower friction

Force and Motion

Brief #3: Gravity

What do you think would happen in the game of baseball if there were no gravity? When a batter hit the ball, it would keep on going and going and going, never falling to the ground.

Focus
Gravity is a pulling force that affects everything in the universe.

Gravity is a pulling force. Gravity pulls everything on Earth towards the ground. You can't smell, taste, or touch gravity, but you can see its affects everywhere. Earth is not the only place where this force exists. **Gravitational force is a force of attraction between all matter and objects in the universe.** The gravitational force is present in everything from atoms to galaxies.

Vocabulary

1. gravitational force

The Strength of Gravity

Gravitational force is not the same everywhere on Earth or in the universe. The strength of the force depends on two things: the mass of the objects and the distance between them. For example, the gravitational force between two large objects only one foot apart is much greater than the force between two small objects 10,000 miles apart.

The table below shows how many meters per second (m/s^2) an object would fall to the center on each of these planets or stars in our solar system.

Acceleration Due to Gravitational Force

Planet/Star	Gravitational Acceleration (m/s_2)
Sun	274.13
Mercury	3.59
Venus	8.87
Earth's moon	1.62
Mars	3.77
Saturn	11.08
Uranus	10.67
Neptune	14.07
Pluto	0.42

An apple would fall to Earth at a rate of 9.8 meters per second.

An apple would fall to Jupiter at a rate of 25.95 meters per second.

Force and Motion

Brief #3: Gravity *(cont.)*

 Tides

The gravitational force on our planet has a huge impact on our oceans. If you have ever observed the ocean where it meets the shore at different times of day you may have noticed that the tides are not always the same. Tides are the rising and falling of the ocean level in the ocean due to gravitational forces between the Earth, sun, and moon.

As the Earth spins on its axis, one part of it faces the moon. Because this portion of the Earth is the closest, the gravitational force is the strongest. Water in the oceans on that moon-facing part of the Earth is drawn towards the moon. This creates a high tide. On the opposite side of the Earth, the water also rises as a high tide as a kind of counterbalance. The parts of the planet that are not experiencing high tide have a low tide.

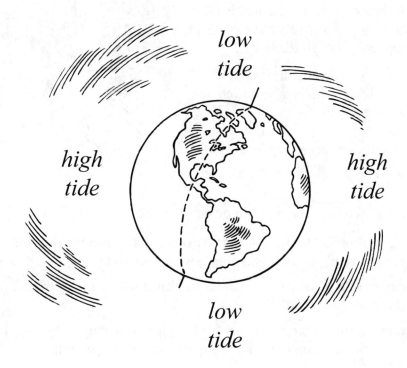

Force and Motion

Brief #4: Motion

How did you get to school today? Did you get a ride in a car or bus? Perhaps you rode your bike or walked to school. No matter how you got here, at some point you were in motion.

Right at this moment you are probably sitting behind your desk. Are you moving? You may say "No," but the truth is that you are moving very quickly. Because the Earth is spinning on its axis and revolving around the sun, you actually never stop moving.

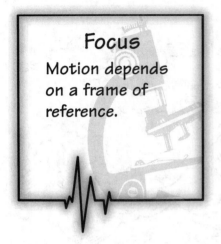

Focus

Motion depends on a frame of reference.

Vocabulary

1. circular motion
2. uniform motion
3. vibratory motion
4. speed
5. velocity
6. acceleration

 ### Motion and Relativity

In order to describe any type of motion, you need to use a frame of reference. A frame of reference is an object that allows you to compare motion.

For example, let's say that you are sitting in a seat on a train and reading a book. If you use your seat and book as a frame of reference, you could say that, relative to your seat and book, you are not moving. This is because everything around you appears to be motionless.

But what would you think if your frame of reference changed? If your frame of reference was the ground outside of the train, then the seat and the book on the train would appear to be whizzing through space very quickly!

 ### Types of Motion

There are many different ways in which objects can move:

✓ **Circular motion is the motion that travels around a central point.** Planets and moons have circular motion. So does a wheel and axle.

✓ **Uniform motion** is the motion that keeps object moving in a straight line. Trains and planes have uniform motion.

✓ **Vibratory motion** is the rapid back-and-forth movement of objects. The strings on a guitar have vibratory motion. Vibratory motion creates sound.

Force and Motion

Brief #4: Motion *(cont.)*

 Describing Motion

Any kind of motion can be described by calculating its speed, velocity, and acceleration.

✓ **Speed**

Speed is a measure of how fast an object moves over a given amount of time. For example, if you travel 200 kilometers in 5 hours, it means that you have traveled at an average speed of 40 kilometers per hour.

The formula for calculating average speed is by dividing the distance traveled by the time you would need to move that distance:

$$\text{average speed} = \frac{\text{distance}}{\text{time}} = 200 \div 5 = 40 \text{ km/h}$$

Let's say that you can ride your bike 5 miles in 20 minutes. To calculate how many miles you could ride in one hour, use the same formula:

$$\text{Average speed} = \frac{\text{distance}}{\text{time}} = \frac{5 \text{ miles}}{20 \text{ minutes}} \text{ x } \frac{60 \text{ minutes}}{1 \text{ hour}} = 15 \text{ mph}$$

Instantaneous speed is the speed of any object at any moment. The speedometer on a car measures instantaneous speed.

✓ **Velocity**

Velocity is the measurement of the speed and the direction of an object. For example, you may ride your bike 20 mph west to get to the grocery store and then ride back home at 20 mph east.

✓ **Acceleration**

Acceleration is a measurement of how velocity changes over time. For example, as you ride your bike to the grocery store at a rate of 20 mph west, you may need to apply the brakes at some point during your trip or speed up at other points. These would be examples of acceleration.

Force and Motion

Brief #4: Motion *(cont.)*

 ### Distance-Time Graph

A distance-time graph can display data about the speed of an object over a given amount of time. The data table below shows how many meters an object travels in a certain number of seconds. The distance-time graph shows the data contained in the table.

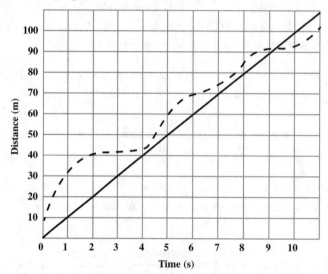

A straight line shows that the object moves at a constant speed. What do you think the broken line on the above graph indicates about the speed of the object?

 ### Speed-Time Graph

A speed-time graph can display data about the speed of an object over a given amount of time.

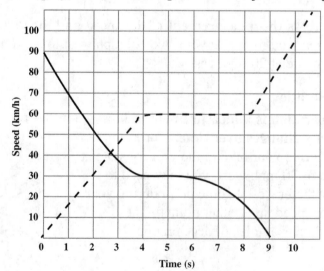

Look at the broken line on the graph above. The diagonal portion shows constant acceleration. The horizontal portion shows constant speed. Look at the solid line. The curved portion shows a change in acceleration.

Force and Motion

Brief #5: Newton's Laws of Motion

Sir Isaac Newton was a scientist who lived in the 17th century in England. In 1686 he published a book called *Principia*. In this book, he describes how motion and force are connected. He outlined three basic laws of motion.

He did not discover these things, but he was the first scientist to fully explain the behavior of forces and motion. Sir Isaac Newton is considered one of the most important scientists who ever lived.

Sir Isaac Newton

 First Law of Motion

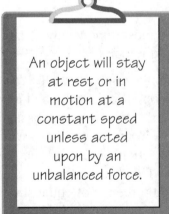

An object will stay at rest or in motion at a constant speed unless acted upon by an unbalanced force.

You can easily demonstrate the first part to this law right at your desk. Place a pencil in front of you. You can see that it is just resting there on your desk. And if no force acts on it, it will continue to rest there forever. But if you push the pencil off of the desk, it will fall to the ground. Your hand pushing the pencil is the unbalanced force that has acted on the pencil.

But what about the second part of Newton's first law? Imagine throwing a baseball. You can predict with 100% accuracy what will eventually happen to the ball. It will fall to the ground because of the force of gravity. But what if we threw that ball out in space where there is no gravity?

Newton's first law states that the ball would keep going and going at a constant speed unless another force came along and acted upon it.

Vocabulary

1. inertia
2. momentum

This law of motion is often called the law of inertia. **Inertia means that an object tends to resist a change in its motion.** In other words, an object at rest will tend to stay at rest, and an object in motion will tend to stay that way too unless some force comes along to change it. The more mass an object has, the greater its inertia.

Force and Motion

Brief #5: Newton's Laws of Motion*(cont.)*

 Second Law of Motion

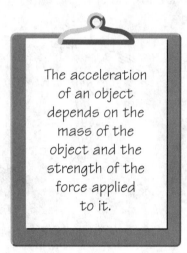

The acceleration of an object depends on the mass of the object and the strength of the force applied to it.

To understand Newton's second law, let's pretend that you are grocery shopping with a friend in preparation for a large party. You both are pushing shopping carts. In your cart you have all of the paper and plastic goods: the plates, napkins, forks, knives, and spoons. In your friend's cart are 10 cases of canned soda. Who has to push harder to get the cart to move forward? If you guessed your friend, then you are correct.

Newton's second law can be described as an equation: **acceleration = force ÷ mass.** When the force on an object increases, its acceleration will increase. When the force on an object decreases, its acceleration will decrease.

 Third Law of Motion

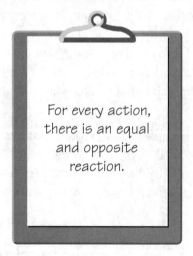

For every action, there is an equal and opposite reaction.

This is probably Newton's most famous law of motion. It means that forces are found in pairs.

Let's imagine that you are playing basketball. You are accelerating toward the hoop, dribbling the ball as you go. When you get about one foot away from the basket, you prepare to jump and shoot. Your feet push down against the ground. This is called the action force. But the ground is also exerting an upward force. This is called the reaction force. The action and the reaction force are of equal strength.

 Momentum

Momentum is related to Newton's third law. **Momentum can be described as the motion of mass.** All matter has mass. If that mass is moving, it also has momentum. Momentum depends upon the object's mass and velocity. Momentum can be described as an equation: **momentum = mass x velocity**. If an object has a large mass and velocity, it has large momentum.

Newton's third law tells us that if we wanted to stop an object with a lot of momentum, then we would need a force that was equal to or greater than the momentum of the object.

Force and Motion

Multiple-Choice Assessment

Name: _____ **Date:** _____

Directions: Read each question carefully. Fill in the correct answer circle.

1. What is a force?
   - Ⓐ momentum
   - Ⓑ velocity
   - Ⓒ acceleration
   - Ⓓ a push or a pull

2. Which is an example of an action-at-a-distance force?
   - Ⓐ friction
   - Ⓑ gravity
   - Ⓒ contact forces
   - Ⓓ all of these

3. What do newtons measure?
   - Ⓐ the size of a force
   - Ⓑ the gravity of a force
   - Ⓒ the direction of a force
   - Ⓓ the net forces

4. The amount of force needed to move one kilogram one meter every second is called a
   - Ⓐ joule.
   - Ⓑ reaction force.
   - Ⓒ newton.
   - Ⓓ net force.

5. Net forces are
   - Ⓐ all the different forces acting on an object.
   - Ⓑ contact forces acting on an object.
   - Ⓒ action-at-a-distance acting on an object.
   - Ⓓ momentum forces.

Force and Motion

Multiple-Choice Assessment *(cont.)*

6. If there is a 15 N force pushing a ball to the right and a 7 N force pushing it in the opposite direction, then what is the net force acting on the ball?

  Ⓐ 22 N to the right

  Ⓑ 105 N to the left

  Ⓒ 2.14 N to the right

  Ⓓ 8 N to the right

7. Which force slows things down?

  Ⓐ gravity

  Ⓑ friction

  Ⓒ electricity

  Ⓓ magnetism

8. When an object at rest begins to move, what kind of friction results?

  Ⓐ static

  Ⓑ rolling

  Ⓒ inertia

  Ⓓ sliding

9. What determines how much friction is present?

  Ⓐ the distance of the object from each other

  Ⓑ the strength of the magnetic force

  Ⓒ what the objects and surfaces are made of

  Ⓓ none of these

10. Friction produces

  Ⓐ heat.

  Ⓑ momentum.

  Ⓒ inertia.

  Ⓓ velocity.

Force and Motion

Multiple-Choice Assessment *(cont.)*

11. The lower the coefficient,

    Ⓐ the higher the friction.

    Ⓑ the lower the friction.

    Ⓒ the higher the gravitational force.

    Ⓓ the lower the gravitational force.

---

12. The mass of objects and the distance between them affects the

    Ⓐ coefficient.

    Ⓑ rolling friction.

    Ⓒ vector.

    Ⓓ gravitational force.

---

13. To describe motion, you need to have a

    Ⓐ frame of reference.

    Ⓑ reference of frame.

    Ⓒ frame of motion.

    Ⓓ frame of relativity.

---

14. When an object is moving in a straight line, what kind of motion does it have?

    Ⓐ circular motion

    Ⓑ vibratory motion

    Ⓒ linear motion

    Ⓓ uniform motion

---

15. Sound is produced by

    Ⓐ uniform motion.

    Ⓑ tubular motion.

    Ⓒ vibratory motion.

    Ⓓ all of these

Force and Motion

Multiple-Choice Assessment *(cont.)*

16. If the speed of a car is 5 miles in 6 minutes, how many miles will it have covered in one hour?

    Ⓐ 55 mph

    Ⓑ 30 mph

    Ⓒ 5 mph

    Ⓓ 50 mph

17. What does velocity measure?

    Ⓐ speed and direction

    Ⓑ speed only

    Ⓒ direction only

    Ⓓ vectors quality

18. If a car is traveling 40 mph west and then travels 30 mph south, it has had a change in

    Ⓐ velocity.

    Ⓑ acceleration.

    Ⓒ speed.

    Ⓓ none of these

19. The tendency for an object to resist a change in its motion is called what?

    Ⓐ an unbalanced force

    Ⓑ momentum

    Ⓒ inertia

    Ⓓ all of these

20. Which of the following would have the greatest inertia?

    Ⓐ a baseball

    Ⓑ a DVD

    Ⓒ a microwave oven

    Ⓓ a cell phone

Force and Motion

Multiple-Choice Assessment *(cont.)*

21. What does Newton's second law of motion relate to?

Ⓐ the acceleration of objects

Ⓑ the inertia of objects

Ⓒ the momentum of objects

Ⓓ the friction of objects

22. What equation describes the second law of motion?

Ⓐ force = mass x inertia

Ⓑ acceleration = force ÷ mass

Ⓒ acceleration = force x mass

Ⓓ acceleration = mass x velocity

23. Mass x velocity =

Ⓐ acceleration

Ⓑ net forces

Ⓒ speed

Ⓓ momentum

24. What must an object have in order to have momentum?

Ⓐ gravity

Ⓑ inertia

Ⓒ motion

Ⓓ none of these

25. If the following objects were rolling at the same speed, which would have the greatest momentum?

Ⓐ a bowling ball

Ⓑ a tennis ball

Ⓒ a ping pong ball

Ⓓ a rolling basketball

Force and Motion

Sentence-Completion Assessment

Name: _____ **Date:** _____

Directions: Read each statement carefully. Fill in the word or words that best complete the sentence.

1. A force is a _____ or a _____.

2. Objects do not have to be in contact for there to be an _____ force in effect.

3. _____ are a measurement of the size of a force.

4. One newton is equal to the force needed to move a one kilogram object the distance of _____ every second.

5. _____ are all of the forces that are acting on an object.

6. The force of _____ slows things down.

7. When an object at rest begins to move, _____ friction results.

8. The amount of friction present depends on how _____ the objects are pressed together.

Force and Motion

Sentence-Completion Assessment *(cont.)*

9. The wheels of a car produce _____ friction.

10. _____ are used in machines to reduce friction.

11. Gravitational force is affected by the _____ of objects and their

_____ from each other.

12. To describe motion, you need to use a _____ of _____ .

13. _____ motion describes motion that moves in a straight line.

14. _____ motion produces sound.

15. A car traveling at the speed of five miles in six minutes will travel _____ miles in one hour.

16. _____ measures both speed and direction.

17. The tendency for an object to resist change is called _____ .

18. The more _____ an object has, the greater the inertia.

Force and Motion

Sentence-Completion Assessment *(cont.)*

19. The acceleration of objects is described in Newton's _____ law of motion.

20. The equation for the second law of motion is _____ =

_____ ÷ _____

21. Mass x _____ = momentum.

22. Newton's third law of motion says that "for every _____ ,

there is an equal and opposite _____ .

23. The motion of mass is also called _____ .

24. A force has both size and _____ .

25. Ocean tides are affected by the _____ force.

Force and Motion

True-False Assessment

Name: _____ **Date:** _____

Directions: Read each statement carefully. If the statement is true, put a **T** on the line provided. If the statement is false, put an **F** on the line provided.

_____ **1.** A force is a push or a pull.

_____ **2.** Gravity is a contact force.

_____ **3.** Newtons measure momentum.

_____ **4.** One newton is equal to the force it takes to move a kilogram one meter in one second.

_____ **5.** All of the forces acting on an object are called net forces.

_____ **6.** Friction speeds things up.

_____ **7.** Static friction results when an object at rest begins to move.

_____ **8.** Magnetism affects friction.

_____ **9.** Friction produces heat.

_____ **10.** The lower the coefficient, the lower the friction.

_____ **11.** The gravitational force is affected by the mass of objects and their distance from each other.

_____ **12.** A frame of reference is needed to describe motion.

Force and Motion

True-False Assessment *(cont.)*

_____ **13.** "Uniform motion" means that an object is moving in a straight line.

_____ **14.** Sound is produced by circular motion.

_____ **15.** A car that travels five miles in six minutes can travel 65 miles per hour.

_____ **16.** Velocity measures speed and direction.

_____ **17.** *Inertia* means that objects resist changes in momentum.

_____ **18.** A bus would have less inertia than an apple.

_____ **19.** Newton's second law of motion describes the acceleration of objects.

_____ **20.** Acceleration = force ÷ mass.

_____ **21.** Momentum = mass x speed.

_____ **22.** The greater the mass, the greater the momentum.

_____ **23.** Ocean tides are affected by friction.

_____ **24.** Forces come in pairs.

_____ **25.** Increased force equals decreased acceleration.

Machines

Matching Assessment

Name: _____ **Date:** _____

Directions: Read the items in both lists below and on page 184 carefully. Choose an item from List B that best matches an item from List A. Write the corresponding letter from List B on the line. You will have some left over.

List A	List B
_____ 1. a push or a pull	**A.** high coefficient
_____ 2. contact force	**B.** vibratory
_____ 3. example of action-at-a-distance force	**C.** force ÷ mass
_____ 4. measurement of force	**D.** acceleration
_____ 5. net forces	**E.** straight line
_____ 6. force that slows things down	**F.** instantaneous
_____ 7. when movement begins	**G.** gravitational force
_____ 8. friction	**H.** tides
_____ 9. low friction	**I.** three
_____ 10. mass and distance	**J.** Isaac Newton
_____ 11. useful to describe motion	**K.** come in pairs
_____ 12. uniform motion	**L.** force

GO

Force and Motion

Matching Assessment *(cont.)*

List A	List B
_____ 13. motion that makes noise	**M.** heat maker
_____ 14. speed and direction	**N.** static friction
_____ 15. inertia	**O.** velocity
_____ 16. relating to 2nd law of motion	**P.** Jupiter
_____ 17. 2nd law equation	**Q.** distance ÷ time
_____ 18. momentum equation	**R.** lubricant
_____ 19. forces	**S.** rolling
_____ 20. number of motion laws	**T.** frame of reference
_____ 21. friction reducer	**U.** all forces on object
_____ 22. car wheel friction	**V.** tendency to resist motion
_____ 23. changes in ocean levels	**W.** low coefficient
_____ 24. speed formula	**X.** mass x velocity
_____ 25. speed at any moment in time	**Y.** newton
	Z. touching objects
	AA. friction
	BB. gravity

Force and Motion

Graphic Assessment

Name: _____ **Date:** _____

Directions: Draw three illustrations that depict the three different types of motion. Name each type of motion and include other labels where necessary.

Motion I

Motion II

Motion III

STOP

Force and Motion

Short-Response Assessment

Name: _____ **Date:** _____

Directions: Read each question carefully. Write a short response of a few sentences to each question.

1. Explain the force of friction. What different types of friction are there? How does friction impact your daily life?

   _____

   _____

   _____

   _____

2. Explain the difference between contact forces and action-at-a-distance forces. Provide an example of each type of force.

   _____

   _____

   _____

   _____

3. Which force affects the oceans' tides? Briefly explain how this happens.

   _____

   _____

   _____

   _____

4. Choose one of Newton's laws of motion and describe it. Provide a real-life example.

   _____

   _____

   _____

   _____

STOP

Technology

Teacher Materials

 ### Teacher Preparation

Before you begin each unit, photocopy and distribute the following to students:
- Student Introduction (page 190)
- Unit Vocabulary (page 191)
- Student Briefs (pages 192–199)
- Appropriate Assessments (pages 200–212)

 ### Key Unit Concepts

- Technology always brings both positive and negative outcomes.
- The negative outcomes of technology are often unforeseen.
- Improvements in transportation and communications have transformed societies.
- Pollution, congestion, and death are some of the negative consequences of current transportation technology.
- Electricity changed communication in the 19th century.
- *Wireless technology* uses electromagnetic waves.
- The development of computer technology began in the 1930s and 1940s.
- The first commercially used computer was UNIVAC in 1951.
- Early computers were large and impractical.
- The *microchip* made smaller computers possible.
- The *World Wide Web* was developed in England as a means for scientists to communicate with one another.
- *Cybercrime* is a negative consequence of the Internet.
- Robots are machines that can help people do work.
- Robots are dependent on computer technology.
- Robots can perform tasks that are too dangerous for people or require a level of delicacy that humans don't have.
- There are different types of robots.
- *Nanotechnology* rearranges atoms and molecules to create new materials.
- *Carbon nanotubes* are very strong.
- Nanotechnology is promising but is not without risk.

 ### Discussion Topics

- Brainstorm a list of all of the technology contained within your house. What could not have been there 20 years ago. What do you think will be there 20 years from now?

See "Generic Strategies and Activities" on pages 8 and 9 for additional strategies useful to presenting this unit.

Technology

Activities

 Brief #1: Transprotation and Communication

- **Make an Illustrated Timeline:** Using a large piece of butcher paper, make an illustrated timeline of the advancements in transportation over the past 200 years. Have your timeline go up to the year 2050 and create an imaginary form of transportation that currently does not exist.

- **Make a Data Table:** Make a data table that shows the top 10 most traffic-congested cities in the United States. Include information on the average time of a typical commute for each location.

- **Create a Public Service Announcement:** Create a two-minute public service announcement that educates the public about automobile safety. Include information about infants, pets, seat belts, cell phones, or substance abuse. Record your commercial and share it with students in other grades.

- **Make an Informational Poster:** Make a poster that shows the alphabet in Morse code.

   Key Words: *developments in transportation, traffic congestion, automobile safely, Morse code*

 Brief #2: Computers and Robots

- **Write a Research Brief:** Write a one-page report that outlines how people your age can be safe while using the Internet. Make sure to include information about social networking sites, cyber-bullying, and any other issues that you think are important.

- **Write a Song, Poem, or Rap:** Research some of the most famous fictional robots (R2D2, Wall-E, etc.) and write a song or poem that tells about them.

- **Research and Report:** Isaac Asimov was a famous and influential science fiction author. Research his Three Laws of Robotics. Add any new laws that you think should be included.

- **Design a Robot:** Invent a new type of robot that helps you in some way. Give your robot a name and draw a detailed illustration of what it looks like and how it will operate. Describe in detail the types of tasks your robot will perform. Tell what the negative consequences of your new robot could be.

- **Simulate Remote Control:** Have students create an obstacle course on the school grounds. Have one student pretend to be a rover. This student should be blindfolded. Have another student who is not blindfolded accompany him/her for safety. Have other students navigate that person verbally around the obstacle course by using simple commands (e.g., turn right, step up, etc.). Have students repeat the exercise to see how repetition helps the blindfolded student navigate the course.

   Key Words: *Internet safety, Isaac Asimov, fictional robots, Three Laws of Robotics*

Technology

Activities *(cont.)*

 Brief #3: Nanotechnology

- **Make a Model:** Using straws, toothpicks, wire, jellied candies and other materials, have student make models of carbon nanotubes and buckyballs.

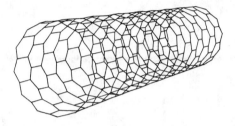 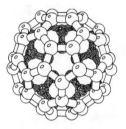

carbon nanotube　　　　　　　　　　　　　*buckyball*

- **Research and Report:** Research the possible future applications of nanotechnology. Investigate the areas of food, medicine, construction, and electronics. Prepare and deliver an oral presentation on the topic. Include any visual material that you think will make your presentation more engaging.

- **Invent a New Material:** Invent a new material that is produced using nanotechnology. What is the name of this new material? What problem does it solve? Create an illustration of the material and some of it applications.

 Internet Resources

- *http://marsprogram.jpl.nasa.gov/funzone_flash.html* — link to the Mars Exploration website from NASA; includes games and activities for students

- *http://robonaut.jsc.nasa.gov/index.asp* — NASA's Robonaut website; includes photos and videos of robots at work

- *http://online.nanopolis.net/* — link to Nanopolis, a site about nanotechnology

- *http://www.nanonet.go.jp/english/kids/* — link to "Nanotech Kids," a student-friendly site that uses animation to explain nanotechnology

Technology

Student Introduction: Technology Word Web

Directions: Use this word web to help you brainstorm characteristics of technology.

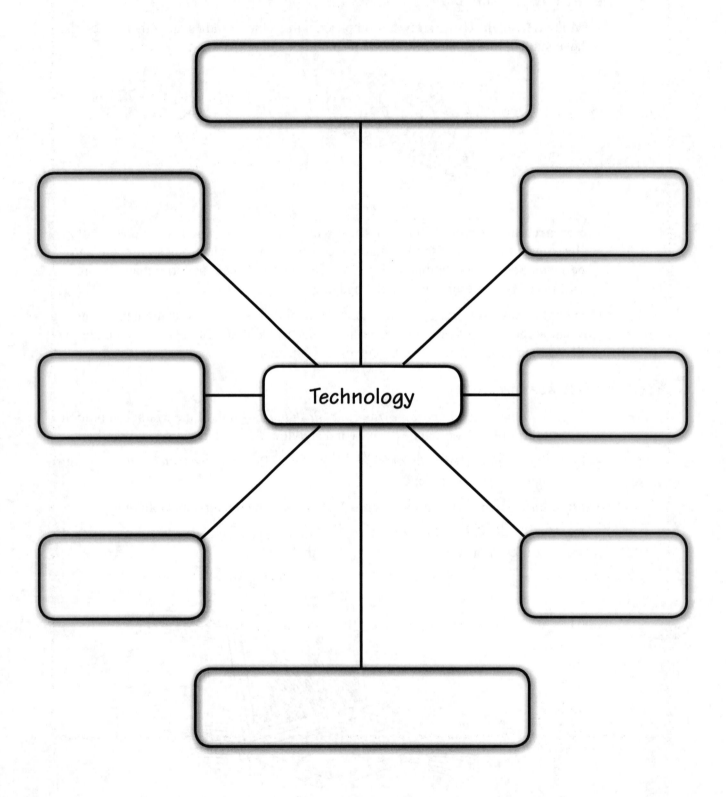

Technology

Vocabulary

1. **autonomous robot**—robot that can perform tasks without human guidance

2. **carbon nanotube**—form of carbon where the atoms are arranged in six-sided rings that form tubes

3. **industrial robot**—factory robot that can do many different tasks at the same time

4. **microchip**—microscopic integrated circuit that can process lots of information

5. **nanotechnology**—the rearrangement of atoms and molecules to produce new materials

6. **robot**—machine that can collect information from the environment and perform work

7. **robotics**—study, design, and manufacture of robots

8. **ROV**—remote-operated vehicle; a robot that is controlled remotely by humans

9. **telecommunications**—system of communications that uses receivers and transmitters to send and receive electronic signals

10. **vehicle**—container that carries people and goods from one place to another

11. **World Wide Web (www)**—communications system that links computers on a global level

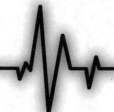

Technology

Brief #1: Transportation and Communication

Focus

Technology is any tool created by people for a purpose.

On April 18th 1775, Paul Revere rode on horseback from Boston to Lexington and Concord to warn the townspeople that the British were coming. Paul Revere's famous ride required both transportation and communication.

Vocabulary

1. vehicle
2. telecommunications

Imagine if Paul Revere had 21st-century technology way back in the 18th century. He may have driven his car from Boston to Lexington and Concord. Maybe he would have just stayed put and sent the townspeople text messages and e-mails warning them of the coming invasion.

People of every age have needed to get from place to place and to communicate with one another. Each age invents news ways to do this, and the technology that currently exists is possible because of the inventions, discoveries, and advancements of the past.

 ### Transportation

A vehicle is any kind of container that is used to transport people and goods from one place to another. Planes, trains, cars, and even space shuttles are all examples of vehicles.

Over the course of many, many centuries, vehicles have developed and changed. They will continue to change as demand creates the need for news kinds of transportation technologies.

Fast Fact

The wheel was invented around 3500 B.C.E. by the ancient Mesopotamians.

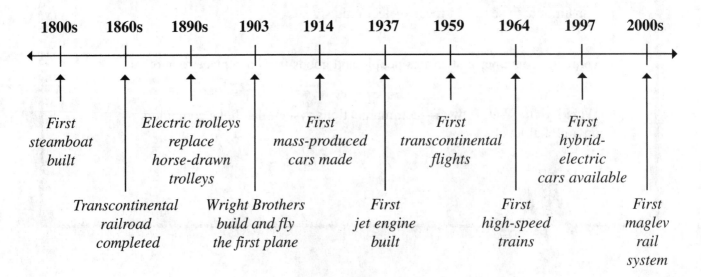

| 1800s | 1860s | 1890s | 1903 | 1914 | 1937 | 1959 | 1964 | 1997 | 2000s |

First steamboat built

Transcontinental railroad completed

Electric trolleys replace horse-drawn trolleys

Wright Brothers build and fly the first plane

First mass-produced cars made

First jet engine built

First transcontinental flights

First high-speed trains

First hybrid-electric cars available

First maglev rail system

Technology *(cont.)*

Brief #1: Transprotation and Communication *(cont.)*

 ### Problems Caused by Transportation

All of the advancements in transportation have revolutionized the world. People and the goods they need to survive and thrive can get from place to place more easily.

But every new technology can bring with it negative consequences. Sometimes these consequences can be predicted and we can prepare for them. But in many, many cases, we cannot foresee the bad things that can happen with the use of a new technology.

One of the biggest problems that our current modes of transportation cause is pollution. Planes, cars, and trucks use gasoline, which is a fossil fuel, for energy. As gasoline is burned inside of the engines of vehicles, pollution leaves the vehicles though the exhaust pipe and pours out into the environment.

Over the years, new technologies have been made to help reduce this pollution, but it is still a big problem. Also, most scientists agree that the exhaust from cars, buses, and trucks contribute to global warming.

Fast Fact

About 40,000 people die every year in the United States in auto accidents.

Traffic congestion is a big problem caused by automobiles. There are over 250 million cars and trucks in the United States alone! In regions and areas that are densely populated, traffic jams are commonplace. Traffic congestion can often make driving very difficult. It can take a person a long time to get to where they are going. Also, traffic jams are a major contributor to pollution. Millions of gallons of gasoline are used every year by people just waiting in traffic.

 ### Communications

Communication means sharing information with another person. Ancient people chiseled words and messages into rocks. Later, people dipped the tips of quills into ink and wrote on paper.

In the 15th century, Johannes Gutenberg invented a technology called the printing press, which completely changed how people shared information. Before the printing press, books had to be copied by hand. The new press meant that books could be produced more easily. As a consequence, the population at the time became better educated. This had an effect on every part of society and culture.

Fast Fact

The typewriter was patented in 1868.

Technology *(cont.)*

Brief #1: Transprotation and Communication *(cont.)*

 ### Telecommunications

In the 19th century, communications underwent an enormous transformation. It was then that communications and the new technology of electricity became linked. Telecommunications is a system that uses receivers and transmitters to send electronic signals for the purpose of communication. Satellites, radios, televisions, and telephones are all examples of telecommunications.

One of the first pieces of electronic technology was invented by Samuel Morse. It was called a telegraph machine. It used wires strung along a series of telegraph poles. A message was tapped out in code and transmitted at one end. The coded message traveled electronically through the wires to a receiver at the other. The first electronic telegraph message was sent from Washington, D.C., to Baltimore, Maryland, in 1844.

telegraph

Telecommunication has come a long way. Currently, many people use wireless technology. Cell phones, laptops, and hand-held computers operate on a wireless network that uses electromagnetic waves to send and receive communications.

1860s	*Pony Express begins*
1870s	*Edison invents first copying machine*
1870s	*Bell patents the telephone*
1880s	*Berliner patents the gramophone*
1890s	*First telephone answering machines*
1902	*First radio signals transmitted*
1923	*Television invented*
1920s	*First "talking" motion picture*
1940s	*First computers used*
1980	*Portable cassette player invented*
1990s	*First commercial digital cameras*

Technology (cont.)

Brief #2: Computers and Robots

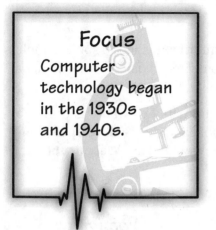

Focus

Computer technology began in the 1930s and 1940s.

It is probably hard to imagine a world without computers, but not that long ago that is how the world was. Nowadays, computers are used in almost every area of our lives: agriculture, education, entertainment, exploration, and medicine.

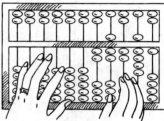

abacus

Some say the world's first "computer" was invented thousands of years ago. It is called an abacus. An abacus is often made of a bamboo frame, and it contains many beads strung on wires. This ancient tool is often called the world's first computer because it was a technology that helped people to perform calculations.

Electronic Computer Technology

As early as the first part of the 20th century, scientists attempted to develop a technology that could perform complex mathematical calculations.

The first electronic computers were gigantic. They took up whole rooms and weighed thousands of pounds. They were not very practical. The first computer that was used commercially was called UNIVAC. UNIVAC stood for Universal Automatic Computer. It was built in 1951. The computer was 25 feet by 50 feet in length. It contained over 5,000 tubes. This enormous first computer could only store 1,000 words!

An important invention in the 1950s revolutionized computer technology and made it much more practical. This invention ultimately made it possible for people to hold computers in their hands. It is called the microchip. **A microchip is a tiny integrated circuit that can process information very quickly.** The circuits on a microchip are so small, they are microscopic.

Vocabulary

1. microchip

Personal Computers

In the late 1970s, personal computers were introduced into the marketplace. These computers were small enough and easy enough to use that they became practical for people to own in their homes.

In the early 1980s, computers became even more practical with the introduction of laptop computers. These were smaller and more portable, allowing the user to carry these devices with them. When they were first introduced, however, these computers were very expensive.

Since then, the technology behind personal computers has advanced at such a rate that incredibly powerful computers that fit in the palm of the user's hand have become increasingly affordable.

Technology (cont.)

Brief #2: Computers and Robots (cont.)

 ### World Wide Web

In the 1960s, '70s, and '80s, computers were used to store information and to solve complex problems very quickly. But it wasn't until the 1990s that computers would transform global communications.

In the 1980s, there was an English scientist named Timothy Berners-Lee who was trying to figure out a way to communicate more efficiently with his colleagues. **He developed the communications system that would come to be called the World Wide Web, or the Internet.**

The Internet has made it possible for people globally to share information with one another in a matter of seconds. It has made it easy to find information and to learn new things. But just like with many new technologies, the Internet has had some negative unintended consequences.

One of these consequences is that there is a lot of misinformation on the Internet. And because communication is almost instantaneous, that misinformation can spread far and wide in a matter of minutes.

Other problems with the Internet involve cybercrime. Identity theft, fraud, and computer hacking to spread viruses are all major problems with the Internet. The Internet has also been used as a tool by some adults to prey on children.

Vocabulary

2. World Wide Web
3. robots
4. robotics
5. industrial robot
6. remotely operated vehicle (ROV)
7. autonomous robot

 ### Robots

When you think of a robot you may think of your favorite science fiction movie. But robots are real and because of computer technology, they perform many specialized jobs for people.

A robot is a machine that can collect information from its environment and perform work. For example, a robot may be used on an automotive assembly line to perform a particular task, like turning a screw into a nut. Robots run by using computer technology, including microchips and processors. As computer technology has advanced, so has robotics. **Robotics is the study, design, and manufacture of robots.**

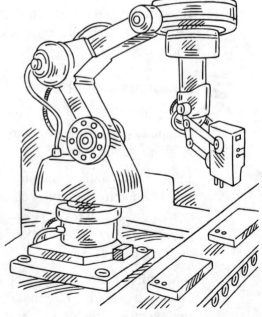

Technology *(cont.)*

Brief #2: Computers and Robots *(cont.)*

 Medicine

Robots are often used in the field of medicine. They are used to transport medicine and supplies from one area of a hospital to another. Robots are often used to help doctors when they perform surgery. Robotic hands, which are controlled by a surgeon, can perform certain operations that are very delicate and require the kind of precision that a human hand cannot provide.

 Industry and Exploration

An industrial robot is a robot that can do many different tasks at the same time. Most industrial robots work in factories. Many of these types of robots do work that was once performed by people. Industrial robots lift, carry, weld, paint, pack, and assemble.

A robot called a *remotely operated vehicle* (ROV), sometimes called a rover, is often used in space exploration. NASA has sent several of these types of robots or rovers to Mars. Robots are often used to perform work that is too dangerous for people or to go to places where people cannot go. A ROV is actually controlled by a human being back on Earth. The robot and the person send signals back and forth to each other. The human decides where the rover will go and how fast it can move.

An autonomous robot is also used in space exploration. **An autonomous robot is a robot that can perform tasks without human guidance.** These robots can make decisions about where to go and how fast to move. They are equipped with sensors that can gather information about atmosphere, temperature, etc. They have cameras that can record information visually.

Technology *(cont.)*

Brief #3: Nanotechnology

Focus

Nanotechnology is one of the world's newest technologies.

You have already learned that the smallest structures on Earth are atoms and that different arrangements of atoms produce about 100 basic elements. **Nanotechnology is a technology that deals with materials on an atomic and molecular level.** A nanometer is a unit of length equal to one billionth of a meter.

In nanotechnology, atoms and molecules are rearranged to create new materials. Nanotechnology is at the beginning of its development, but scientists think that it will have many useful applications as it develops.

Vocabulary

1. nanotechnology

2. carbon nanotube

In order to make new materials this way, scientists will require very specialized robots that are able to pick up atoms and move and rearrange them in very specific ways. Also, in order to make a new material, robots will have to pick up and move billions and billions of atoms. Lots of robotic arms would be needed to complete a task this size. For this reason, not that many new materials have been created by nanotechnology, but scientists are working to overcome some of these issues.

Uses of Nanotechnology

Because nanotechnology is so new, scientists are still learning about how it can be applied or used in everyday life. One new material that has been produced is called a nanopore. If nanopore material is put in water that is polluted with mercury or lead, the material will absorb these toxic substances.

Nanoshells may be able to help people fight cancer without the use of chemotherapy. A nanoshell can be injected into a cancerous tumor. The nanoshells attach themselves to the cancer cells. Infrared light superheats the nanoshells, which in turn destroy the cancer cells. Healthy tissue around the tumor is unharmed.

Technology *(cont.)*

Brief #3: Nanotechnology *(cont.)*

 Carbon Nanotubes

Carbon is one of the elements. But there are a few different types of carbon. The differences between these forms of carbon is the way the carbon atoms are arranged. Diamond, graphite, and amorphous carbon are forms of carbon. There is another type of carbon called a buckyball. A buckyball is made of 60 carbon atoms.

Another form of carbon was discovered in the 1990s. This form is called a carbon nanotube. **A carbon nanotube is a carbon molecule where the atoms are arranged in six-sided rings that form a tube.**

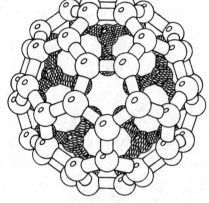

buckyball

Carbon nanotubes are stronger than steel but only one-sixth the weight of steel. They can be both good conductors of electricity and heat. Scientists think that carbon nanotubes may be useful in the future in the areas of building, medicine, and electrical circuitry.

Like all technologies, nanotechnology will have both positive and negative consequences. When atoms are rearranged to form new materials, they can become unstable. This means that they have the potential to become toxic and harmful to people and the larger environment. As nanotechnology progresses, scientists will have to monitor developments very carefully to make sure that the benefits of this new technology outweigh the risks.

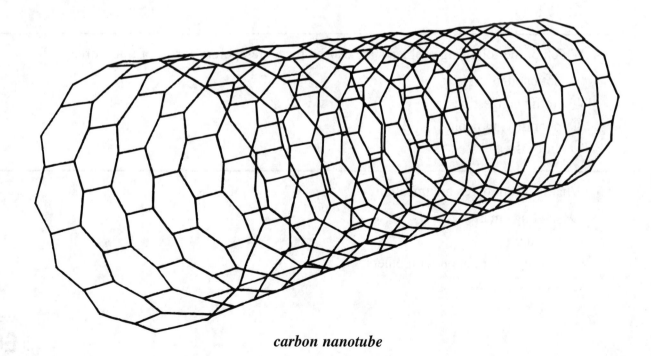

carbon nanotube

Technology

Multiple-Choice Assessment

Name: _____ **Date:** _____

Directions: Read each question carefully. Fill in the correct answer circle.

1. About how long ago was the wheel invented?

    Ⓐ 3,000 years ago

    Ⓑ 1,000 years ago

    Ⓒ 10,000 years ago

    Ⓓ 6,000 years ago

_____

2. Which of the following is a vehicle?

    Ⓐ car

    Ⓑ boat

    Ⓒ bike

    Ⓓ all of these

_____

3. In what century was the transcontinental railroad completed?

    Ⓐ 19th

    Ⓑ 18th

    Ⓒ 20th

    Ⓓ 17th

_____

4. Which of the following problems are caused by contemporary forms of transportation?

    Ⓐ not enough cars

    Ⓑ traffic congestion

    Ⓒ poor driving habits

    Ⓓ all of these

_____

5. What is meant by communication?

    Ⓐ sending email

    Ⓑ talking

    Ⓒ sharing information with others

    Ⓓ writing letters

Technology

Multiple-Choice Assessment *(cont.)*

6. In what century did Gutenberg invent the printing press?

   Ⓐ 16th

   Ⓑ 15th

   Ⓒ 10th

   Ⓓ 17th

---

7. How did the printing press impact society?

   Ⓐ food production

   Ⓑ transportation

   Ⓒ literacy

   Ⓓ none of these

---

8. Telecommunications uses

   Ⓐ receivers and transmitters.

   Ⓑ code.

   Ⓒ telegraph poles.

   Ⓓ moveable type.

---

9. What had a major impact on the development of telecommunications?

   Ⓐ fossil fuel

   Ⓑ nuclear power

   Ⓒ the car

   Ⓓ electricity

---

10. What was the first computer developed for?

    Ⓐ to store information

    Ⓑ to help scientists from different parts of the world communicate

    Ⓒ to perform calculations

    Ⓓ all of these

Technology

Multiple-Choice Assessment *(cont.)*

11. What was UNIVAC?

    Ⓐ the name of the fist mass produced car

    Ⓑ the name of the first computer used in space

    Ⓒ the name of the first computer that used the Internet

    Ⓓ the name of the first commercially used computer

12. When was UNIVAC built?

    Ⓐ 1951

    Ⓑ 1961

    Ⓒ 1981

    Ⓓ 1941

13. What was one of the great disadvantages about UNIVAC?

    Ⓐ It was huge.

    Ⓑ It was very inaccurate.

    Ⓒ It created a lot of pollution.

    Ⓓ It was hard to fix.

14. What invention made it possible for computers to become much smaller?

    Ⓐ the robot

    Ⓑ nanotechnology

    Ⓒ carbon nanotubes

    Ⓓ the microchip

15. What does "WWW" stand for?

    Ⓐ World Wide Wisdom

    Ⓑ World With Web

    Ⓒ World Wide Web

    Ⓓ World Wide Wavelengths

Technology

Multiple-Choice Assessment *(cont.)*

16. Where was the Internet first developed?

  Ⓐ England

  Ⓑ the United States

  Ⓒ Russia

  Ⓓ Japan

---

17. Why was the Internet originally developed?

  Ⓐ for use in the military

  Ⓑ to help scientists communicate with each other

  Ⓒ to reduce terrorism

  Ⓓ all of these

---

18. What is a robot that works in a factory called?

  Ⓐ an autonomous robot

  Ⓑ a rover

  Ⓒ an assemblebot

  Ⓓ an industrial robot

---

19. What does "ROV" stand for?

  Ⓐ robotically operated vehicle

  Ⓑ remotely operated vehicle

  Ⓒ remotely operated vessel

  Ⓓ robot originated vehicle

---

20. How is an ROV controlled?

  Ⓐ by hundreds of microchips

  Ⓑ it controls itself

  Ⓒ by sensors on the wheels

  Ⓓ humans using remote control

Technology

Multiple-Choice Assessment *(cont.)*

21. A robot that can perform tasks without human guidance is called

Ⓐ an autonomous robot.

Ⓑ an industrial robot.

Ⓒ a smartbot.

Ⓓ none of these

---

22. What can some types of robots do?

Ⓐ play sports

Ⓑ perform surgery

Ⓒ work as cooks

Ⓓ reproduce themselves

---

23. Nanotechnology is involved with

Ⓐ using bacteria to cures diseases.

Ⓑ using microchips to build structures.

Ⓒ rearranging atoms and molecules to produce new materials.

Ⓓ all of these

---

24. How are diamonds, graphite, and buckyballs similar?

Ⓐ They are all made of hydrogen.

Ⓑ They are all elements that are combustible.

Ⓒ They were all discovered in the 20th century.

Ⓓ They are all made from carbon atoms.

---

25. What makes carbon nanotubes unique?

Ⓐ They are stronger than steel but weigh much less.

Ⓑ They weight almost nothing.

Ⓒ They are indestructible.

Ⓓ all of these

Technology

Sentence-Completion Assessment

Name: _____   **Date:** _____

Directions: Read each statement carefully. Fill in the word or words that best complete the sentence.

1. The wheel was invented _____ years ago.

2. A container that transports people or goods is called a _____ .

3. The transcontinental railroad was completed in the _____ century.

4. Cars and buses cause pollution and _____ congestion.

5. Sharing information with others is also called _____ .

6. Gutenberg invented the printing press in the _____ century.

7. Before the printing press, books had to be reproduced by _____ .

8. Telecommunications requires _____ and transmitters.

9. The first computers were developed to help perform _____ .

10. The first commercially used computer was called _____ .

11. The first commercially produced computer, the UNIVAC, was built in the year _____ .

12. The invention of the _____ enabled computers to be made much smaller.

Technology

Sentence-Completion Assessment *(cont.)*

13. "WWW" stands for _____ .

14. The Internet was first developed in the country of _____ .

15. The _____ was developed to help scientists communicate with each other.

16. A robot that works in a factory is called an _____ robot.

17. "ROV" stands for _____ .

18. ROVs are operated by using _____ control.

19. A robot that can perform tasks without human guidance is called an _____ robot.

20. An _____ robot can perform many tasks at the same time.

21. The rearrangement of atoms and molecules is called _____ .

22. A _____ is a type of molecule made of 60 carbon atoms.

23. A nanometer is one _____ of a meter.

24. A _____ is made of six-sided rings.

25. A nanoshell may be able to help people fight _____ .

Technology

True-False Assessment

Name: _____ **Date:** _____

Directions: Read each statement carefully. If the statement is true, put a **T** on the line provided. If the statement is false, put an **F** on the line provided.

_____ **1.** The wheel was invented about 6,000 years ago.

_____ **2.** A vehicle moves people and goods from place to place.

_____ **3.** The transcontinental railroad was completed in the 20th century.

_____ **4.** Traffic congestion and pollution are problems with nanotechnology.

_____ **5.** Communication was not as necessary in the 19th century as it is today.

_____ **6.** The Gutenberg press was invented in the 17th century.

_____ **7.** The printing press helped to educate the masses.

_____ **8.** Receivers and transmitters are used in telecommunications.

_____ **9.** Electricity had a big impact on communication in the 19th century.

_____ **10.** The first computers were developed to control space exploration.

_____ **11.** UNIVAC was the first commercially used computer.

_____ **12.** UNIVAC was developed in the 1960s.

Technology

True-False Assessment *(cont.)*

_____ **13.** A disadvantage of UNIVAC was its size.

_____ **14.** The invention of the microchip completely changed computer technology.

_____ **15.** "WWW" stands for World Wide Web.

_____ **16.** The Internet was developed in Japan.

_____ **17.** The Internet was developed originally as a way for the military to monitor terrorism.

_____ **18.** An industrial robot usually works in a factory.

_____ **19.** "ROV" stands for "Robot Optical Vehicles."

_____ **20.** An ROV is remotely controlled by humans.

_____ **21.** An autonomous robot can perform tasks without human guidance.

_____ **22.** Robots can work with doctors to perform surgery.

_____ **23.** *Nanotechnology* is another word for robotics.

_____ **24.** A buckyball is made of 60 carbon atoms.

_____ **25.** Carbon nanotubes are incredibly strong.

Technology

Matching Assessment

Name: _____ **Date:** _____

Directions: Read the items in both lists below and on page 210 carefully. Choose an item from List B that best matches an item from List A. Write the corresponding letter from List B on the line. You will have some left over.

List A	List B
_____ 1. invention of wheel	**A.** atom rearrangement
_____ 2. vehicle	**B.** factory work
_____ 3. 19th century	**C.** space exploration
_____ 4. transportation problem	**D.** mercury
_____ 5. information sharing	**E.** six-sided rings
_____ 6. 15th century	**F.** telecommunications
_____ 7. receivers and transmitters	**G.** Gutenberg press
_____ 8. UNIVAC	**H.** doesn't need human guidance
_____ 9. laptop computers first introduced	**I.** World Wide Web
_____ 10. UNIVAC disadvantage	**J.** electromagnetic waves
_____ 11. microchip	**K.** possible cancer fighter
_____ 12. WWW	**L.** remotely operated vehicle

GO

Energy

Matching Assessment *(cont.)*

List A	List B
_____ **13.** England	**M.** pollution
_____ **14.** industrial	**N.** size
_____ **15.** ROV	**O.** 1 billionth of a meter
_____ **16.** use of ROVs	**P.** the 1980s
_____ **17.** autonomous robot	**Q.** wheel inventors
_____ **18.** nanotechnology	**R.** container that carries goods and people
_____ **19.** buckyball	**S.** integrated circuit
_____ **20.** carbon nanotube	**T.** 60 carbon atoms
_____ **21.** length of nanometer	**U.** 3500 B.C.E.
_____ **22.** nanoshell	**V.** communication
_____ **23.** Mesopotamians	**W.** first commercially used computer
_____ **24.** wireless technology	**X.** transcontinental railroad completed
_____ **25.** robotics	**Y.** cyber crime
	Z. where Web was developed
	AA. study and design of robots

Technology

Graphic Assessment

Name: _____ **Date:** _____

Directions: Select four technologies that you think have had the greatest impact on society. Draw and label an illustration of each.

Technology I

Technology II

Technology III

Technology IV

Technology

Short-Response Assessment

Name: _____ **Date:** _____

Directions: Read each question carefully. Write a short response of a few sentences to each question.

1. The ancient Greek philosopher Plato said, "Necessity is the mother of invention." Explain what you think this phrase means. Provide a few real-life examples that illustrate this idea.

   _____

   _____

   _____

   _____

   _____

2. New technology brings both positive and negative outcomes. What do you think may be some possible positive and negative outcomes of robotics in the future?

   _____

   _____

   _____

   _____

   _____

3. Describe nanotechnology. What are some of the current problems with this technology?

   _____

   _____

   _____

   _____

4. Compare and contrast the invention of the printing press with the invention of the Internet.

   _____

   _____

   _____

   _____

   _____

STOP

Graphic-Assessment Rubric

Category	4	3	2	1
Accuracy	95% of the assigned structures are drawn accurately and are recognizable.	94–85% of the assigned structures are drawn accurately and are recognizable.	84–75% of the assigned structures are drawn accurately and are recognizable.	Less than 74% assigned structures are drawn accurately and are recognizable.
Labels	All items have labels, and it's clear which label goes with what.	94–85% of items have labels, and it's clear which label goes with what.	84–75% of items have labels, and it's clear which label goes with what.	Less than 74% of items have labels, and it's not clear which label goes with what.
Spelling	95% of the words are spelled correctly.	94–85% of the words are spelled correctly.	84–75% of the words are spelled correctly.	Less than 74% of the words are spelled correctly.
Knowledge Gained	95% of the items can be identified accurately.	94–85% of the items can be identified accurately.	84–75% of the items can be identified accurately.	Less than 74% of the items can be identified accurately.
Drawing Details	95% of details have been included and are clear and easy to identify.	94–85% of details have been included and are clear and easy to identify.	84–75% of details have been included and are clear and easy to identify.	Less than 74% of details have been included and are clear and easy to identify.

Short-Response Rubric

Criteria	Possible Points	Score
The response is 4 to 6 sentences long.	25	
The response conforms to the standard conventions of grammar and spelling.	25	
The response answers the questions posed.	25	
The response contains enough details and elaboration to fully answer the question.	25	

Answer Key

Unit #1

Multiple Choice (pages 23–26)

1. A
2. D
3. C
4. B
5. C
6. A
7. B
8. A
9. D
10. A
11. D
12. C
13. B
14. B
15. D
16. B
17. C
18. D
19. A
20. D

Sentence Completion (pages 27–28)

1. 17th
2. microscope
3. cork
4. animalcules
5. theory
6. Multi-cellular
7. organelle
8. vacuole
9. cell membrane
10. mitochondria
11. plant
12. diffusion
13. osmosis
14. divide
15. DNA
16. mitosis
17. Chromosomes
18. cytoplasm
19. 23
20. lysosome

True-False (pages 29–30)

1. T
2. T
3. F
4. T
5. F
6. F
7. T
8. F
9. T
10. T
11. F
12. F
13. T
14. T
15. T
16. T
17. T
18. F
19. T
20. F

Answer Key (cont.)

Matching (pages 31–32)

1. U
2. S
3. D
4. C
5. I
6. V
7. T
8. L
9. H
10. N
11. P
12. O
13. M
14. E
15. J
16. B
17. G
18. R
19. Q
20. A

Graphic (page 33)

Compare answers to chart on page 22. Consult rubric on page 213.

Short Response (page 34)

1. Cell theory explains what cells are and where they come from. Cell theory states that all living things are made of cells, cells are the basic units of living things, and all cells come from existing cells. Cell theory has evolved over time. Because cells are too small to be seen by the naked eye, the inventions of better and more powerful microscopes have led to an increasing understanding of cells. This progress should only continue as our scientific technology improves.

2. Give students credit for all well-supported answers.

3. Cells use two different processes to move molecules in and out of the cell through the membrane. In a cell, substances move from an area of high concentration to an area of low concentration by process called *diffusion*. When there is the same amount of molecules on the inside as on the outside of a cell, the cell is in a state of equilibrium. Diffusion can take place with any kind of molecules that pass through the cell membrane. Osmosis works the same way as diffusion, but osmosis only refers to the movement of water.

4. *Mitosis* means that the cell nucleus, which contains the DNA, divides. The DNA coils and forms tubular structures called chromosomes. During mitosis, the nucleus of each new cell receives a full set of chromosomes. Mitosis is complete when the cytoplasm divides, so from one cell two new identical cells are produced.

Unit #2

Multiple Choice (pages 49–53)

1. D
2. D
3. D
4. C
5. A
6. C
7. B
8. D
9. B
10. A
11. D
12. C
13. B
14. A
15. C
16. B
17. A
18. D
19. D
20. B
21. A
22. D
23. A
24. C
25. C

Sentence Completion (pages 54–55)

1. asexual
2. sexual
3. fission
4. budding
5. fragmentation
6. egg
7. sperm
8. chromosomes
9. meiosis
10. egg, sperm
11. zygote
12. pollen
13. stamen
14. pistil
15. DNA
16. double helix
17. genes
18. A, T, G, C

Answer Key *(cont.)*

19. base pairs
20. GC or CG
21. traits
22. mitosis
23. mutation
24. dominant
25. hybrid

True-False (pages 56–57)

1.	T	14.	T
2.	F	15.	T
3.	F	16.	F
4.	T	17.	T
5.	F	18.	T
6.	T	19.	T
7.	F	20.	F
8.	T	21.	F
9.	F	22.	T
10.	F	23.	F
11.	T	24.	T
12.	F	25.	T
13.	F		

Matching (pages 58–59)

1.	H	14.	M
2.	K	15.	S
3.	P	16.	I
4.	V	17.	D
5.	G	18.	O
6.	X	19.	Z
7.	E	20.	C
8.	W	21.	U
9.	L	22.	Y
10.	R	23.	A
11.	B	24.	J
12.	F	25.	T
13.	Q		

Graphic (page 60)

Py	Py
Py	Py

OO	WO
OW	WW

Short Response (page 61)

Answers will vary. Consult rubric.

1. Asexual reproduction means that the offspring of a living organism comes from a single parent and has the exact DNA as the parent. There are four different types of asexual reproduction: fission, budding, spore formation, and fragmentation. During fission, an organism splits into two identical organisms; each new organism can grow to the same size as the original organism. Bacteria are reproduced through fission. In budding, a single parent forms a smaller version of itself that sprouts from its own body. Smaller organisms, such as hydra, reproduce by budding. Some types of plants, algae, and fungi reproduce through spore formation. During this process, a tiny cell with a protective coating is produced on the plant; when the weather is right, the spore breaks open and tiny spores are released.

Finally, fragmentation occurs when a new organism is grown from a part of the parent. If a sea star or worm is cut apart, a new and identical organism can grow from the pieces.

2. *Meiosis* is the process in which sex cells are produced. During meiosis, a single sex cell is divided and produces four new cells. Each new cell only has half the chromosomes of the parent. So an egg cell has 23 chromosomes, and a sperm cell has 23 chromosomes.

3. DNA is a chemical molecule that is located in the cells of all living things. DNA is made up of four different chemical bases: A, T, G, and C. The genes in DNA are made up of base pairs, such as the base pair GC. Each rung of the DNA is made up of two base pairs. Bases C and G can only form pairs with each other, and bases A and T can only form pairs. DNA is in the shape of a double helix, which looks like a twisted ladder.

4. Traits can be either dominant or recessive. A dominant trait can be seen in the offspring, while a recessive trait is not seen. Which traits appear in the offspring is determined by how the parents' gene pairs are formed. For example, if two people each have one dominant gene for brown eyes and one recessive

gene for blue eyes, their child would be born with BB, Bb, or bb. With the BB and Bb combination the child would be born with the dominant trait of brown eyes, but with the bb combination, the child would be born with the recessive trait of blue eyes.

Unit #3

Multiple Choice (pages 74–77)

1. C
2. B
3. A
4. C
5. D
6. A
7. A
8. B
9. D
10. D
11. C
12. A
13. C
14. B
15. D
16. C
17. B
18. D
19. A
20. C

Sentence Completion (pages 78–79)

1. roots
2. nutrients, water
3. epidermis
4. hairs
5. xylem
6. phloem
7. stem
8. leaves
9. stomata
10. guard cells
11. transpiration
12. chlorophyll
13. photosynthesis
14. chlorophyll
15. glucose
16. cellular respiration
17. angiosperm
18. gymnosperm
19. germination
20. tropism

True-False (pages 80–81)

1. T
2. F
3. T
4. F
5. F
6. T
7. F
8. F
9. T
10. F
11. F
12. F
13. T
14. F
15. T
16. T
17. T
18. F
19. T
20. F

Matching (pages 82–83)

1. Q
2. K
3. M
4. D
5. P
6. R
7. I
8. B
9. L
10. S
11. F
12. W
13. V
14. T
15. N
16. G
17. C
18. O
19. J
20. E

Graphic (page 84)

Check graphic for accuracy and understanding. Consult rubric on page 213.

Short Response (page 85)

Answers will vary. Consult rubric.

1. Photosynthesis is the process that plants use to make food. Plants take in carbon dioxide, water, and light. Those ingredients are combined with chlorophyll, and as a result, glucose and oxygen are produced. Cellular respiration enables plants to change a surplus of glucose into other sugars and starches that can be stored and used when needed. In cellular respiration, glucose is broken down into the cells; oxygen then moves through the cells and continues to break the substances down into smaller materials. Finally, carbon dioxide, water, and energy are

Answer Key (cont.)

released into the organism. The two are known as opposite processes because they take the same elements to form two completely opposite equations. Each process forms the energy the other process needs to make their equation complete.

2. Tropism is a behavior found in plants. It means that a plant is growing toward or away from something in its environment. There are several types of tropism, and each type responds to a different environmental element. *Heliotropism* responds to the sun, hydrotropism responds to the water, *thermotropism* responds to the temperature, and *graviotropism* responds to gravity.

3. Vascular plants grow from seeds. Once the seed of a vascular plant is in the ground it can begin to germinate. The germination process begins in the soil at the roots. Vascular plants can germinate as either angiosperms or gymnosperms. Angiosperms are flowering plants. The seeds are fertilized after pollination. Angiosperms rely on bees and birds to carry the pollen between plants to produce new seeds. Gymnosperms are vascular plants that produce cones, and the seeds of these plants are found in these cones. The pollen of the cones is carried from the male cones to the female cones on the wind. After the female cones have been fertilized, they close so the seeds can mature. When they are ready, the cone reopens and the seeds fall to the ground.

4. Plants and animals need each other to survive. During the process of photosynthesis, plants produce oxygen as a by-product. Animals take in this oxygen as they inhale. When animals exhale, they release carbon dioxide, which in turn is taken up by plants. This is called the carbon dioxide-oxygen cycle. Without plants, animals would not have the oxygen they need to survive on Earth.

Unit #4

Multiple Choice (pages 98–101)

1.	A	11.	D
2.	C	12.	D
3.	D	13.	B
4.	C	14.	D
5.	D	15.	D
6.	C	16.	B
7.	A	17.	C
8.	B	18.	C
9.	D	19.	B
10.	B	20.	A

Sentence Completion (pages 102–103)

1. crust
2. 25
3. mantle
4. core
5. liquid
6. iron
7. lithosphere
8. scientific theory
9. empirical
10. Pangaea
11. continental drift
12. sea-floor spreading
13. magnetic field
14. plate boundary
15. divergent
16. transform
17. fault
18. parasitic cone
19. ash cloud
20. top

True-False (pages 104–105)

1.	T	11.	T
2.	T	12.	T
3.	F	13.	F
4.	F	14.	T
5.	T	15.	F
6.	T	16.	T
7.	F	17.	T
8.	T	18.	F
9.	F	19.	F
10.	T	20.	T

Matching (pages 106–107)

1. R
2. S
3. J
4. E
5. T
6. D
7. I
8. V
9. F
10. M
11. O
12. U

Answer Key *(cont.)*

13. L
14. H
15. C
16. Q
17. G
18. N
19. W
20. B

Graphic (page 108)

Check graphic for accuracy and understanding. Consult rubric on page 213.

Short Response (page 109)

Answers will vary. Consult rubric.

1. Wegener's theory of continental drift explains how the Earth's continents came to be in their current locations. Wegener believed that at one time, millions and millions of years ago, all of the continents were joined together in one super continent called Pangaea. Empirical evidence to support Wegener's theory includes the shape of the continents and the fossil records. His theory explained why the same plants and animals lived along the eastern coast of South America and the western coast of Africa. Wegener's theory did not explain how the continents had actually moved to their current positions.

2. Empirical evidence is evidence based on experience or observation. Empirical evidence is a necessity in scientific investigation because it is used to confirm a theory.

3. The lithosphere is the crust of the Earth, as well as its upper mantle. The lithosphere is a collection of large pieces of solid rock. These giant pieces of crust and mantle are called plates. The plates are not the same size as the continents. Whole continents and vast oceans can rest on top of a single plate. The lithosphere floats on top of the liquid part of the mantle.

4. Hot magma from the Earth's mantle pushes up through the part of the Earth's crust that is beneath the ocean. As magma flows up and out, it cools off and forms new crust. This new crust pushes the old crust aside. This action causes the sea floor to spread apart, which in turn pushes the tectonic plates that the ocean is above to move out. It is the movement of these tectonic plates that is causing the spreading of the sea floor.

Unit #5

Multiple Choice (pages 123–126)

1. D
2. B
3. A
4. B
5. C
6. C
7. D
8. C
9. D
10. A
11. D
12. B
13. A
14. C
15. D
16. B
17. A
18. D
19. D
20. A

Sentence Completion (pages 127–128)

1. atoms
2. electron cloud model
3. negative
4. 18
5. Elements
6. elements
7. nonmetals, metalloids
8. metals
9. families
10. protons
11. periods
12. bonded
13. atoms
14. chemical formula
15. mixture
16. solute
17. solvent
18. concentration
19. acids, bases
20. acid

Answer Key *(cont.)*

True-False (pages 129–130)

1.	T	11.	F
2.	T	12.	T
3.	F	13.	F
4.	F	14.	F
5.	F	15.	T
6.	F	16.	T
7.	T	17.	F
8.	F	18.	T
9.	T	19.	T
10.	T	20.	F

Matching (pages 131–132)

1. I
2. U
3. O
4. E
5. N
6. L
7. H
8. W
9. B
10. P
11. G
12. S
13. C
14. K
15. T
16. R
17. V
18. J
19. D
20. Q

Graphic (page 133)

Check graphic for accuracy and understanding. Consult rubric on page 213.

Short Response (page 134)

Answers will vary. Consult rubric.

1. The periodic table is a big chart that lists all of the elements that are present on Earth. The table is arranged in seven rows and eighteen columns. The elements in the columns are called *families,* and they have certain things in common. The elements in the rows are called *periods,* and they have very little in common. Each element on the table has an atomic number. The atomic number tells how many protons are in the nucleus of each element. Three-quarters of the way across the table there is a zig-zag line. All the elements to the right of the line are non-metals and all the elements to the left are metals. The elements along the zig-zag are called metalloids. The two rows at the bottom of the table are there so the periodic table can appear neatly on one page.

2. A compound is a substance that is produced from the bonding of two or more elements. Every compound that is formed has a certain chemical formula.

   *Give students credit for providing an example of a chemical formula and explaining what that formula means.

3. Mixtures are substances that are not chemically bonded. For example, a fruit salad could be called a mixture. In such a mixture, it would be easy to separate the parts (e.g., grapes, strawberries, pineapple) that make up the mixture. Solutions, though, are mixtures in which you can't see the individual materials that make up the mixture. An example would be if you made a glass of salt water. It would be difficult to see the salt once you stirred it into the water and it dissolved.

4. Everything in the known universe is made up of tiny particles called atoms. Each atom is structured the same way. There is a nucleus in the center, of each atom. The nucleus is filled with the same number of protons (which have a positive electrical charge) and neutrons (which have no electrical charge). Surrounding the nucleus there is an electron cloud. Electrons have a negative electrical charge. There are the same number of electrons as protons and neutrons in the atom. Every atom has a different number of protons in its nucleus. It is this number of protons that gives the atom its atomic number and makes it different from all other atoms.

Answer Key (cont.)

Unit #6

**Multiple Choice
(pages 145–148)**

1. C
2. B
3. D
4. C
5. A
6. D
7. C
8. D
9. B
10. C
11. A
12. A
13. C
14. D
15. C
16. B
17. D
18. C
19. C
20. C

**Sentence Completion
(pages 149–150)**

1. pushing, pulling
2. force, distance
3. joules
4. machine
5. single
6. decrease
7. six
8. screw, pulley, wedge, inclined plane
9. slanted
10. screw
11. wheel, axle
12. wedge
13. lever, wedge, screw or inclined plant (any one)

14. fulcrum
15. three
16. load, fulcrum
17. first-class
18. second-class
19. third-class
20. third-class

True-False (pages 151–152)

1. T
2. F
3. F
4. T
5. T
6. F
7. T
8. F
9. T
10. T
11. F
12. F
13. F
14. T
15. F
16. T
17. F
18. T
19. F
20. T

Matching (pages 153–154)

1. F
2. O
3. I
4. S
5. K
6. C
7. G
8. T
9. R
10. Q
11. P
12. H
13. J
14. L
15. M
16. U
17. A
18. B
19. E

Graphic (page 155)

Check graphic for accuracy and understanding. Consult rubric on page 213.

Short Response (page 156)

Answers will vary. Consult rubric.

1. Three simple machines are the wheel and axel, the wedge, and the pulley. A wedge is two or more inclined planes that come together in a point. Wedges can be used to wedge, or split, materials apart. Wedges can also be used to stop something from moving. A doorstop is an example of a wedge. The doorstop keeps a door from closing.

2. The three types of levers are the first-class, second-class, and third-class lever. In the first-class lever, the effort force and the load are at opposite ends and the fulcrum is in the middle. A crow bar is an example of a first-class lever. In a second-class lever, the effort force and the fulcrum are at opposite ends and the load is in the middle. A nutcracker is a second-class lever. In the third-class lever, the fulcrum and the load are at opposite ends and the force is in the middle. A stapler is a third-class lever.

3. Give students credit for a list that includes six of the simple machines found in your classroom.

4. Give students credit for all well supported answers.

Answer Key (cont.)

Unit #7

Multiple Choice
(pages 173–177)

1. D
2. B
3. A
4. C
5. A
6. D
7. B
8. A
9. C
10. A
11. B
12. D
13. A
14. D
15. C
16. D
17. A
18. A
19. C
20. C
21. A
22. B
23. D
24. C
25. A

Sentence Completion
(pages 178–180)

1. push, pull
2. action-at-a-distance
3. Newtons
4. one meter
5. Net forces
6. friction
7. static
8. tightly
9. rolling
10. Lubricants
11. mass, distance
12. frame, reference
13. Uniform
14. Vibratory
15. 50
16. Velocity
17. inertia
18. mass
19. second
20. acceleration, force, mass
21. velocity
22. action, reaction
23. momentum
24. direction
25. gravitational

True-False (pages 181–182)

1. T
2. F
3. F
4. T
5. T
6. F
7. T
8. F
9. T
10. T
11. T
12. T
13. T
14. F
15. F
16. T
17. F
18. F
19. T
20. T
21. T
22. T
23. F
24. T
25. F

Matching (pages 183–184)

1. L
2. Z
3. BB
4. Y
5. U
6. AA
7. N
8. M
9. W
10. G
11. T
12. E
13. B
14. O
15. V
16. D
17. C
18. X
19. K
20. I
21. R
22. S
23. H
24. Q
25. F

Answer Key *(cont.)*

Graphic (page 185)

circulatory, uniform, vibratory

Check graphic for accuracy and understanding. Consult rubric on page 213.

Short Response (page 186)

Answers will vary. Consult rubric.

1. Friction is a force that is the result of objects pressing tightly against each other. The force of friction slows things down. There are three types of friction: rolling, sliding, and static frictions.

   * Give students credit for all well-supported answers that explain how friction impacts their daily lives.

2. Forces act on all objects in the universe. A force is a push or a pull. Contact forces act only if the objects involved are touching each other. Forces that can act on objects without having to contact them are called action-at-a-distance forces.

   * Give students credit for providing two examples of each type of force.

3. Tides are the rising and falling of the ocean level due to gravitational forces between the Earth, sun, and moon. The gravitational force on our planet has a huge impact on our oceans. As the Earth spins on its axis, one side of it faces the moon. Because this portion of the Earth is closest, the gravitational force is the strongest. Water in the oceans on the moon-facing part of the Earth is drawn towards the moon. This creates high tide.

4. The first law of motion states an object will stay at rest or in motion at a constant speed unless acted upon by an unbalanced force. The second law of motion states that the acceleration of an object depends on the mass of the object and the strength of the force applied to it. The third law states that for every action, there is an equal and opposite reaction.

   * Give students credit for providing a real-life example for all three laws of motion.

Unit #8

Multiple Choice (pages 200–204)

1. D
2. D
3. A
4. B
5. C
6. B
7. C
8. A
9. D
10. C
11. D
12. A
13. A
14. D
15. C
16. A
17. B
18. D
19. B
20. D
21. A
22. B
23. C
24. D
25. A

Sentence Completion (pages 205–206)

1. 6,000
2. vehicle
3. 19th
4. traffic
5. communications
6. 15th
7. hand
8. receivers
9. calculations
10. UNIVAC
11. 1951
12. microchip
13. World Wide Web
14. England
15. Internet
16. industrial
17. remotely operated vehicle
18. remote
19. autonomous
20. industrial
21. nanotechnology
22. buckyball
23. billionth
24. carbon nanotube
25. cancer

Answer Key (cont.)

True-False (pages 207–208)

1. T
2. T
3. F
4. F
5. F
6. F
7. T
8. T
9. T
10. F
11. T
12. F
13. T
14. T
15. T
16. F
17. F
18. T
19. F
20. T
21. T
22. T
23. F
24. T
25. T

Matching (pages 209–210)

1. U
2. R
3. X
4. M
5. V
6. G
7. F
8. W
9. P
10. N
11. S
12. I
13. Z
14. B
15. L
16. C
17. H
18. A
19. T
20. E
21. O
22. K
23. Q
24. J
25. AA

Graphic (page 211)

Check graphic for accuracy and understanding. Consult rubric on page 213.

Short Response (page 212)

Answers will vary. Consult rubric.

1. Give students credit for explaining what they think the phrase means and for providing real-life examples that support their explanation.

2. Give students credit for all well-supported answers, which include both positive and negative outcomes for the use of robotics in the future.

3. Nanotechnology is a technology that deals with materials on an atomic and molecular level. In nanotechnology, atoms and molecules are rearranged to create new materials. Nanotechnology is a fairly new technology, so there are still problems with its development. When atoms are rearranged to form new materials, they can become unstable. This means that they have the potential to become toxic and harmful to people and the larger environment. As scientists become more familiar with this technology, they will hopefully eliminate this problem with it.

4. The printing press was invented in the 15th century, and it completely changed how people shared information. The new press meant that books could be produced easily. As a result, the population at the time became better educated because they now had knowledge available to them. The invention of the Internet was similar in that it allowed people to share information. This time though, people are sharing information within a matter of seconds. People no longer have to wait for a book to get to them, now the information appears before them almost as quickly as they can type. Like the printing press, the Internet has allowed knowledge to be even more readily available, so people can continue to self educate. Unfortunately, with this new technology has come new misuse. There is a lot of misinformation on the Internet, and because of the speed of communication, this misinformation can be spread at a very rapid pace.